AF839277

# Capitalism and the Dark Forces of Time and Ignorance

David Harrison

# Capitalism and the Dark Forces of Time and Ignorance

## Economic and Political Expectations

palgrave macmillan

David Harrison
Sevenoaks, UK

ISBN 978-3-030-78393-8    ISBN 978-3-030-78394-5 (eBook)
https://doi.org/10.1007/978-3-030-78394-5

© The Editor(s) (if applicable) and The Author(s), under exclusive license to Springer Nature Switzerland AG 2021
This work is subject to copyright. All rights are solely and exclusively licensed by the Publisher, whether the whole or part of the material is concerned, specifically the rights of translation, reprinting, reuse of illustrations, recitation, broadcasting, reproduction on microfilms or in any other physical way, and transmission or information storage and retrieval, electronic adaptation, computer software, or by similar or dissimilar methodology now known or hereafter developed.
The use of general descriptive names, registered names, trademarks, service marks, etc. in this publication does not imply, even in the absence of a specific statement, that such names are exempt from the relevant protective laws and regulations and therefore free for general use.
The publisher, the authors and the editors are safe to assume that the advice and information in this book are believed to be true and accurate at the date of publication. Neither the publisher nor the authors or the editors give a warranty, expressed or implied, with respect to the material contained herein or for any errors or omissions that may have been made. The publisher remains neutral with regard to jurisdictional claims in published maps and institutional affiliations.

Cover illustration: © John Rawsterne/patternhead.com

This Palgrave Macmillan imprint is published by the registered company Springer Nature Switzerland AG
The registered company address is: Gewerbestrasse 11, 6330 Cham, Switzerland

# Preface

The theme running through this book is how expectations of the future—a future about which we know very little—affect present-day economic activities, and in particular the function of investment. Expectations are precarious, and rise and fall in line with sentiment in speculative investment markets. When they rise too far, and collapse completely, the collapse in expected yields of capital assets precipitates an economic crisis, a full-scale depression if the investment comes to a full stop, and quite possibly a political crisis too.

Numerous authors have written about the inadequacies of modern economics since the 2008 financial crisis. To name a few, in chronological order: John Cassidy (*How Markets Fail: The Logic of Economic Calamities)* (2009) made the case early on against "utopian economics", and the idea that markets are inherently rational. In *A Failure of Capitalism* (2009) and *The Crisis of Capitalist Democracy* (2010) Richard Posner described how the modern world had until the crisis of 2008 forgotten Keynes, and the lessons of the 1930s. In *Licence To Be Bad: How Economics Corrupted Us* (2019) Jonathan Aldred took to task fifty years of economic theory for undermining moral and ethical behaviour. In *Narrative Economics* (2019) Robert Shiller described how stories—not logic—propel economic events, and in particular events in finance. In *Radical Uncertainty* (2020) John Kay and Mervyn King explained how too much weight has been given to reasoning in terms of probability, and too little to situations where the future is completely unknown.

This book does not come, once again, to bury modern economics. It strives, instead, to praise some thinkers and their ideas which it suggests help explain the modern capitalist world, with its many and patent flaws. Rather than follow every twist and turn of how these ideas have been interpreted, adapted, or explained away by succeeding generations—which would make for a much longer work—it goes back to the root of some original concepts and applies them directly.

The starting point is Keynes's *General Theory of Employment, Interest, and Money* (1936). This is a complex work, and hardly an easy read, but I think it is fair to say that there is not one aspect of modern global capitalism, in all its maddening perplexities, which is not illuminated by it. Time and again, what seem to be today's unique problems, creating today's headlines, turn out to have been foreseen, or at least thought about, by Keynes. As he said in concluding the *General Theory*, it is the potency of ideas for the future which counts.

I have drawn in particular on Keynes's chapters dealing with the marginal efficiency of capital; the state of long-term expectation; the nature of capital; and the trade cycle. (I would suggest, in passing, that the marginal efficiency of capital remains a more useful concept, with greater explanatory power, than the efficient market hypothesis, of more recent and doubtful vintage.)

Since Keynes set such store by expectations in the face of an uncertain future, it is natural to examine what they are. In doing so it helps to consider the wider question of the nature of human knowledge, and the role played by expectations, developed over his many works by Karl Popper. In this way it becomes possible to see how the radical uncertainty which haunts capitalism—the dark forces of time and ignorance—might be illuminated by rationality.

Perhaps surprisingly, this book has a good word to say about Hayek too. Hayek's idea that prices transmit useful knowledge around the economy, like a telecommunications system, still seems to have much going for it—within its limits. Those limits are explored in the book, and were helpfully clarified by Hyman Minsky. And from Minsky there comes the concept of "money manager capitalism"—the form of institutional savings, developed in recent decades in the United States, from which many ills have arisen.

From a financial and economic crisis to a political crisis is but one short step, and many countries in the developed world have taken that step since 2008. When economic expectations collapse, it usually follows that horizons shorten, politics turns inwards and the search for scapegoats takes over from reason and cooperation. This means that the question of putting capitalism on a more rational footing has become synonymous with maintaining the open society itself.

Sevenoaks, UK David Harrison

# Contents

CHAPTER 1

# Living in Truth

**Abstract** Contrasts Hayek's idea in 1945 that prices help create a rational economic order with the speculative financial order which emerged in the latter decades of the twentieth century.

**Keywords** Price signals · Enterprise · Speculation · Decentralised economy · Marginal efficiency of capital

## Professor Hayek's Knowledge Machine

Towards the end of the Second World War the thoughts of many turned to the nature of post-war society. On the one hand, the *laissez-faire* free market economy had been thoroughly discredited by the crash of 1929 and the Great Depression of the 1930s. On the other hand, the Soviet-style Communist economy seemed incompatible with democracy. So should the economy of the future be planned or unplanned?

In September 1945 the economist Friedrich Hayek (1899–1992) put forward a bold new idea, with far-reaching consequences. Writing in an American economic journal, Hayek suggested a centrally planned economy could never work because no central planner could ever have all the knowledge to keep the economy running in the face of constant change. Instead, a *decentralised* economy would be better, with many

© The Author(s), under exclusive license to Springer Nature Switzerland AG 2021

D. Harrison, *Capitalism and the Dark Forces of Time and Ignorance*,
https://doi.org/10.1007/978-3-030-78394-5_1

separate individuals responding individually to shifting circumstances of time and place, and making their own minute adjustments accordingly. Rather than trying to bring all knowledge into one place, and run the economy as if it were a planned scientific programme, subject to command and control, much more limited practical knowledge would suffice—provided this knowledge could get quickly to those who needed it, and at the right time and place.

How could this be done? Hayek's answer was through the price system. Like a system of telecommunications, price signals would carry instant messages of information from one part of the world to another, spreading useful and practical knowledge of changing circumstances to all who need it.

Suppose, said Hayek, that somewhere in the world a new use is found for a commodity like tin—or that a source of supply for tin is cut off. Those producers who use tin do not have to know all the details; all they need to know is that tin has become more expensive and they will have to economise. If some know of a new demand for tin, and switch resources to it, others will fill their place, the effects will spread rapidly through the whole economic system and influence all the uses of tin and its substitutes; the supply of all things made of tin, and their substitutes; and so on. And this entire chain of events will happen without most of those taking part in this process of change having the slightest idea about the original cause of it.

Hayek wrote of the "marvel" of the price system in bringing about all these adjustments, moving tens of thousands of people in the right direction, without any order being issued. And Hayek meant something deeper than just adjustments in the tin price. What is being brought together is real *knowledge*, dispersed non-scientific practical knowledge, beyond the reach of any individual (or any central planner) but knowledge of the kind necessary to allow society to function. By the price system a division of labour and coordinated use of resources based on an equally "divided knowledge" is all made possible. Hayek likened it to a telecommunications system, but the title of his article was "The Use of Knowledge in Society". The problem he was addressing was nothing less than the best way to construct a rational economic order.

In September of 1945, when Hayek published his piece, the future shape of the post-war world was far from obvious. In 1944, only the year before, delegates at the United Nations Monetary and Financial Conference, meeting in Bretton Woods in the United States, had agreed a treaty setting out the rules for global financial cooperation and reconstruction.

In the spirit of the wartime alliance, even the Soviet Union sent a delegation. Weeks before Bretton Woods, the Allied landings in Normandy began the liberation of occupied Europe, and forces moved in gradually from the west as Soviet forces moved in gradually from the east.

In 1945 the immediate problem in Europe was not so much the rational order of society as its very survival. By the end of the war the scale of physical destruction was massive; civilian deaths and casualties were significant fractions of national populations; refugees and displaced persons criss-crossed the continent; and civil and political structures almost everywhere were broken.

Then in March 1946, speaking at Westminster College, Fulton, in the United States, Winston Churchill gave dramatic warning of a new iron curtain descending, from "Stettin in the Baltic to Trieste in the Adriatic", east of which, in the Soviet sphere, Moscow-led Communist parties were taking control (speech, "The Iron Curtain"). In 1947, by now fearing complete economic catastrophe, the United States inaugurated the Marshall Plan, which, through the Organisation for European Economic Cooperation, aimed to revive the moribund European economies.

It was at this point that Hayek's distinction between centrally planned and decentralised economies came into its own. The Soviet Union refused to allow countries under its control in central and eastern Europe to participate in the Marshall Plan. Instead, in 1949 it created the Council on Mutual Economic Assistance (CMEA or Comecon), to coordinate national economic plans across the Soviet region.

In western Europe, market economies were reconstituted along decentralised lines, first through national reconstruction and investment, boosted by Marshall aid, and then by integration of the individual national economies into a larger-scale European market. This process began with the sectors of coal and steel through the European Coal and Steel Community of 1951, and during the course of the 1950s and 1960s was extended to all other economic sectors through the launch of a European common market, via one of the two Treaties of Rome of 1957.

The object of this exercise was to merge separate national markets into one large European market "constituting a powerful unity of production" (as it was put in one of the founding documents), with an increased division of labour eliminating the waste of resources and allowing larger-scale industries to operate across Europe, without monopolies. It was accepted that this process would take time—decades—and to ensure the market rules were obeyed a central institution—the European Commission—would need to enforce them, and also competition policy, and prohibit distorting subsidies by member states to their own industries. Over the years—and in fact to this day—the Commission and national competition authorities of the member states have worked together to ensure that producer prices are not distorted by anti-competitive behaviour. The enforcement of tough rules prohibiting price-fixing between competitors, and abuses of their market position by firms in a dominant position, has become the hallmark of European competition policy, to which companies all around the world pay careful attention.

All this falls under the heading of a decentralised economy, in the language of Hayek's 1945 article. There is no central plan in western Europe. There are instead the countless individual plans of tens of thousands of firms competing among themselves, producing according to price signals undistorted by anti-competitive behaviour, to encourage a better international division of labour.

Meanwhile, the Soviet-led centrally planned system of central and eastern Europe developed along very different lines. In the CMEA there was no role for decentralised prices. From the late 1940s onward most industry in central and eastern Europe came under the control of the state. Each country adopted a five, or six, year economic plan. Within these plans, the gap between known levels of production of goods and services was compared with the plan targets ("known demand"), and an estimate made how to fill the gap. Estimates were passed down to industry ministries, and within them down to industrial directorates, and eventually down to the enterprises under their control. Enterprises, for their part, drew up provisional plans for their own divisions and plants, which were passed back up the planning chain. The overall planning estimate was adjusted in the light of these reports, and the exercise repeated, sometimes only completed *after* the year to which the plan applied. Planning documents could run to thousands of pages. Hayek's price-signalling telecommunications system had no role to play: planning relied on quantities instead of prices, and the information moving through the system was slow, inaccurate and out of date, by no means getting to the right place at the right time.

Trying to combine each centrally planned economy in a regional European planned system made life even harder. Each centrally planned economy aimed to develop in the same way, favouring heavy industry by importing coal, iron ore, and staple foodstuffs while exporting iron, steel, and machinery. The Soviet Union became the heart of the CMEA, controlling from Moscow a radial pattern of trade and economic activity across central and eastern Europe. Annual plans for cross-border volume flows of goods were drawn up by national state authorities, with planners in each CMEA member state implementing import and export quotas and fixing border prices, basing them on average world prices over a five-year period. Some limited specialisation emerged: the Soviet Union imported car parts from other CMEA countries and exported finished cars; Hungary had a monopoly on the production of buses; Romania the right to produce diesel locomotives.

The rigidities and inefficiencies of the CMEA system became gradually manifest over time. By the 1960s male mortality rates in central and eastern Europe began to rise, while continuing to decline in the west. A steep rise in global oil prices after the suspension of the Bretton Woods currency arrangements in the 1970s put ultimately fatal strains on European Communism, leading to its eventual collapse. The Soviet Union cut back on subsidised oil to other CMEA countries, and Poland, Hungary and the GDR in particular ran up enormous US dollar-denominated debts with international commercial banks to pay for imported western industrial and consumer goods. In 1985 Gorbachev arrived in power in the Soviet Union, with a policy of restructuring the Soviet economy. However, his attempts at reform, involving the introduction of market measures into the centrally planned economy, led to political liberalisation and the eventual secession from the Communist system by CMEA countries, and finally the dismantling of the Soviet Union itself.

In 1990 the newly elected first President of post-Communist Czechoslovakia, Václav Havel, surveyed the damage done by the experiments of the previous forty years. In his New Year's Day address on assuming office, Havel remarked how, when flying to Bratislava, he had looked out onto the industrial complex of the Slovneft chemical plant, plus a giant housing complex right behind it. The view was enough for him to understand that for decades statesmen and political leaders had not looked out of their own aircraft windows: no study of statistics could have enabled him to understand the legacy of forty years faster and better.

Havel's speech can be read as the epitaph on the centrally planned economy. The enormous creative and spiritual potential of the Czech and Slovak nations was being wasted: entire branches of industry were producing goods of no interest to anyone, while the things people needed were lacking. The state, calling itself a "workers' state", humiliated and exploited workers. The outmoded economy wasted what little energy there was. A country once proud of the educational level of its citizens now ranked seventy-second in the world. "We have polluted our land, rivers and forests, bequeathed to us by our ancestors; we now have the most contaminated environment in all of Europe. People in our country die sooner than in the majority of European countries" (speech, "New Year's Address").

By the 1990s, after the collapse of Communism and the centrally planned economies of Europe, there could be no reasonable dispute: the decentralised western European economy worked much better, with prices signalling information rather than the state attempting to control it. As a dissident under the Soviet system, Havel had spoken of "living within the truth"; a simple statement of facts and realities in a Communist regime built on obfuscation and Orwellian doublespeak. In the end, truth prevailed.

So the second half of the twentieth-century vindicated what Hayek had suggested in 1945. Bringing together dispersed knowledge through the price system not only improved the division of labour but made an economy more energy-efficient and less polluting, with better life prospects for workers, producing goods and services that people actually wanted and needed. This lesson that the market system worked seemed of universal significance. Not just in Europe, but on a global scale, the better use of knowledge in society could surely make life better for everyone, everywhere, in a matter of time.

## Not a Time Machine

By the first decade of the twenty-first century the largest markets in the world were not, however, in coal, or steel, or chemicals, or indeed anything that might be produced, or people might consume, or use. Instead, financial products based on underlying goods or services outstripped everything. Foreign exchange trading in currencies had risen to 73 times the value of actual global trade by 2010 (compared to a mere 11 times in 1980). The value of trading in oil futures grew from 20% of global physical oil production and consumption in 1980 to 10 times physical production and consumption by 2010. And there grew out of nowhere a market in devices known as "credit default swaps", allowing two banks or other financial institutions to swap each other's risk of default on the loans each made, or the bonds each held, for a mutually agreed fee. In a matter of a few years in the 1990s these devices had evolved from specialised, bilateral, tailor-made agreements between two parties to mass-produced securities. The gross market value of credit default swaps peaked in 2008, with a total of $5.1 trillion (roughly the same as half the GDP of the European Union).

Behind this market for credit default swaps there came another innovation in the United States: the creation of elaborate new securities based on pooling income streams from mortgages to house-buyers, with ratings based on the riskiness of packages of mortgages. These schemes worked beautifully so long as US house prices moved ever upward, but not when prices started to decline, raising the default risks of impossible-to-identify tranches of "sub-prime" securities, which rapidly became viewed in the market as toxic financial assets.

In 2007 a slide in United States property prices began, leading to a collapse in the market for mortgage-related securities, distress in the US financial sector, the bankruptcy of Lehman Brothers in 2008 and the near breakdown of the entire global financial system. This financial crisis became the worst since the crash of 1929, which had ushered in the Great Depression. Its repercussions were still working their way through the political economy of the developed world a decade and more later.

After the crash of 2008, it was noticed that credit default swap prices, measured in terms of spreads for major banks, had continued to move downwards, reaching a historic low in early summer 2007, so providing no warning at all of impending financial disaster. In other words, one of the largest markets in the world, trading in instruments to capture risk between the world's most sophisticated and knowledgeable financial institutions, had been transmitting signals conveying little or no practical information.

The foreign exchange market, with enormous volumes of trading, far exceeding global trade in real goods and services, might equally have been expected, following Hayek's logic, to convey useful knowledge on a grand scale. That was certainly what some in the market believed when global trading in currencies really took off, in the 1980s. As the head of one large US bank put it at the time, the old Bretton Woods gold standard had now been replaced by an "information standard", based on the huge flows of information running through the trading rooms of the world's global banks, carrying out a non-stop global plebiscite on the currencies issued by governments, and holding them to account. He likened it to a democratic process; as if absolute monarchs were being held in check by the universal suffrage of the markets.

But the results of this global plebiscite, expressed in prices, have been deeply puzzling. In the transatlantic area, bridging the two enormous market economies of the United States and Europe, responsible for about half the world's economic output, the dollar rose by 81% against the German mark in the period from 1979 to 1984; fell by 49% in the period from 1984 to 1987; and then rose by 12% between 1987 and 1988. In the twenty-first century, after the replacement of the German mark by the euro in continental Europe, the euro-dollar price has swung by margins of 15–25% *nine times* in the decade since 2007.

Needless to say, the US and European economies have not expanded and contracted like accordions in the space of ten years. Nor, in the 1980s, did the US economy almost double compared with the German, and then suddenly deflate to half its size. The dollar-euro exchange rate is sometimes called the most important price in the world. If so, it is hard to call whatever it is signalling useful or practical knowledge.

Or take Hayek's own example of the price of tin. As Hayek put it, instant messages conveyed by price signals would allow producers using tin to adjust their plans, and the supply and demand for tin and all its substitutes would move rapidly in line. The actual wholesale price of tin in recent decades, on the other hand, shows general stability in the 1960s (with a low of $2163 per metric ton in May 1960), followed by a rapid increase in prices in the 1970s, a slow decrease in the 1980s and for the remainder of the twentieth century, and then massive volatility in the twenty-first century, with prices hitting an all-time high of $33,265 in 2011 before slumping to below $15,000 in 2016. This tin price pattern is typical of the prices of other basic commodities: crude oil prices have moved up and down in much the same way over these same decades.

So something seems to be missing from the Hayekian explanation of the world. His telecommunications system certainly still exists—information passes around the world today faster than ever, much faster than in 1945. And yet much of the information flashing through the global circuitry seems unreliable and untrustworthy, for anyone who wants to use it to make things, or plan for the future.

What exactly is the knowledge transmitted through the price system? Hayek was describing knowledge that is useful to producers, who need the minimum information about changing circumstances. This is what prices tell them. He linked it to the division of labour in the economy: divided knowledge—dispersed practical knowledge about processes and markets—would come together through the price mechanism and allow resources to be used properly.

It is a producer's-eye view of the world. Producers, in a state of competition with other producers, receive price signals telling them what is going on that is important to the process of production. If what they produce uses tin, they will need to adjust their output, or their designs, or their own prices, in light of what changes in the tin price say.

This knowledge is of something that is already out there, somewhere. The price signals in Hayek's world are telling of what exists, registering changes as they occur and transmitting them to those who need to know. The telecommunications system transmits news—news of events that have occurred, perhaps even of events as they occur, in real time.

But what it is not able to do is transmit news from the future. It cannot tell what has not yet happened. It is for the producer himself to decide the future price of his output. When it comes to setting his own sale price for the future, the producer must make the best judgement he can. And—since this is a decentralised system, with producers competing with one another—he is not allowed to agree that sale price with other producers.

Yet when we look at today's enormous global financial markets they are performing a different function. In one way or other they are trying to provide estimates or forecasts of future events; and prices in these markets are a current view—the current majority view in the market—of what that future will look like. The point of credit default swaps is to insure against the risk of future defaults. And when in 2007 the prices of credit default swaps gave no hint of the impending catastrophe that was because the collective view of the banks involved was that there was no impending catastrophe—until there was one.

In the foreign exchange market the shifting prices of currencies represent the shifting majority opinion within the banking system—which is where nearly all foreign exchange transactions take place—about the future. It is not the relative sizes of the US and European economies which really matter, or the volume of trade between them. What matters at any given moment is the prevailing balance of expectations about the future prospects of one currency compared to another. Prices are volatile because there is never any settled view of the future.

The oil futures market is today much greater than actual oil production and consumption, and there has been huge volatility in the oil price in the twenty-first century. Tin, and other commodities, have followed a similar pattern, with prices moving in correlated patterns according to flows of finance. The "marvel" of the price system has turned into something of a riddle for anyone relying on it.

## Two Views of the Future

What is the best way of seeing into the future? One way is by the scientific method. This is to build objective theories which explain why events arise, and provide forecasts of what will happen in the future. These forecasts must be testable, and theories can be disproved if events do not unfold as predicted—in which case the search will be on for a better theory, which does a better job of explanation.

Through the use of rigorously testable theories much of the future does in fact become predictable. Scientific explanations of the motion of the earth around the sun, and the tilt of the earth, make the seasons predictable. Explaining the revolution of the earth on its own axis makes the change from day to night predictable, and explaining the motion of the moon around the earth makes the changes in the tides of rivers and seas predictable. Science creates a better understanding of the world, and its place in the universe, and man's place in the world, and with each scientific step forward the future becomes that little more comprehensible. Short-term weather forecasts today, based on improving scientific knowledge, are more accurate than they were twenty years ago.

Another way of predicting the future is not scientific at all, and consists of establishing prevailing subjective opinion about the course of future events. This prevailing opinion is changeable, and often amounts to an extrapolation of the recent past into the future. If current events are volatile it is assumed the future will be—if they are calm, the future will be calm. The future is a current poll of what might happen, and by the time it arrives it is less important to have been right than to be part of the majority view then of future events yet to happen.

This method is not completely irrational, and prevailing opinion must have some plausible explanation, story, or narrative to give it force; but because it is not rooted in a testable theory it can vacillate quickly, and swing from one story to another, quite possibly contradictory, one. Prevailing opinion can be optimistic, or pessimistic; and disappointments or pleasant surprises can make sentiment change in short order. Nor is extrapolation supported by strict logic. Extrapolating from recent experience into the future, assuming that because things have happened in the past they will do so again, rests only upon custom and habit and psychology, as Scottish Enlightenment philosopher David Hume pointed out in 1739, almost three hundred years ago.

The enormous financial markets which dominate the global economy of the twenty-first century are driven by a mixture of these two methods. There is usually a foundation, or basis, of a scientific method and above that a vast shifting sea of sentiment and opinion, fluctuating back and forth with elastic ties to what is actually known, beneath.

The extension of credit to buy houses through individual mortgages, for example, is rooted in a reasonably scientific method. A careful assessment is normally made of the creditworthiness of a borrower, and the value of the property against which a mortgage is offered. Different banks or mortgage lenders might have different standards, but there is nothing random about the process. It is when many individual mortgages have been pooled together (or "securitised"), and mortgage-backed securities become tradable (and therefore valued) wholesale against other mortgage-backed securities—and securities which have nothing to do with mortgages—that the underlying predictability of the scientific method is lost. The opinion, or best guess, of the market as a whole becomes the dominating factor. As in 2007, it can be blind to the future.

The foreign exchange markets have as their basis a critical analysis—which could also be called scientific—of the individual countries issuing currencies. This includes important factors like the strength of an economy and its political system, the balance of trade, the rate of inflation, and the level of public indebtedness. But this is only a starting point. Since these factors hardly change for most countries from one period to the next they do nothing to explain the turbulence of the foreign exchange markets.

What drives these markets are shifting expectations of the future. Usually it is the interest rate applying to a particular currency which is the key factor, and expectations relate to prospective differentials in interest rates between two, or more, currencies. The market will value a currency where the prospects of earning a higher rate of interest from holding it appear better—until such a point where it seems expensive against other currencies with different prospects. There is no equilibrium to be arrived at here—just constantly shifting opinion, only loosely connected to the underlying economies.

At a fundamental level the stock market is valuing the prospective stream of income from holding shares in a company. This too is capable of precise analysis, involving careful study of the history of a company, its products and its place in the market, and its future prospects. Some investors and financial analysists pride themselves on knowing a company better than those managing it. But at a wholesale level, the prices of individual company stocks rise and fall against each other for reasons having little to do with the individual merits of the companies concerned, and more to do with collective expectations of different economic sectors, entire economies, and linkages between one company and another—or between one stock market and another.

In the 1930s, the economist John Maynard Keynes (1883–1946) drew a distinction between those operators in the stock market who attempt to make estimates of the long-term yields of capital assets (which he called "enterprise"), and those in the stock market who attempt to forecast the psychology of the market (which he called "speculation"). The former is akin to a scientific method: the yield of capital assets is calculable, in general and with respect to any particular company. There is ample evidence and data about yields to be able to create a reasonable theory that yields in future should be within a given range. It is no great mystery.

Forecasting the psychology of the market ("speculation") is another matter altogether. The problem is, as Keynes pointed out, that this activity comes to predominate as markets become bigger, and more "liquid" (that is, easy to trade shares back and forth). It can be much easier, and more lucrative, for professional investors to try to foresee market developments a short time ahead, and move money accordingly, than to stick to a long-term strategy, irrespective of rises and falls in the share price.

We have come a long way here from living in truth. Keynes characterised speculative markets as being governed by doubt rather than by conviction; by fear more than by forecast; by memories of last time and not by foreknowledge of next time. This kind of emotional group dynamics is far removed from any scientific method, whose aim is to establish actual knowledge.

Why does this matter? For one thing, the accumulated savings of the world are riding on stormy seas. There has been a seemingly inexorable growth in pooled and managed savings, rising from some $11 trillion in 1990 to $87 trillion in 2014 (about the same size as global GDP) and a projected $100 trillion by 2020. If these savings are not productively invested for the long term they cascade, speculatively, from one asset class to another.

It has become also a volatile closed financial system, encircling the global economy, communicating mostly with itself. Completely different parts of it interconnect. Panic in the international bond market following the collapse of the Russian financial system led to the near collapse and bailout in New York of the hedge fund Long-Term Capital Management in 1998. Falling house prices in Florida in 2007 led to the spectacular near breakdown of the global financial system in 2008. The US stock price index has been seen to track the movement of the US dollar: the Korean equity market to track the Hungarian equity market.

The feedback effects of the mutterings and chatterings of this system quite easily turn to alarm, as in 1998 and 2008. Where doubt and fear are the prevailing sentiments, it does not take much to trigger panic. There are, also, severe consequences for associated real-world economic and political structures, most obviously when there is a visitation in the form of a financial crash, pulling down everything connected to it. The economic shock impact of the global crash of 2008 has been likened to that of a war and, not surprisingly, those around the world who did not cause it but suffered the consequences became massively resentful. Polarisation and political extremism have grown everywhere since 2008.

The dark forces of time and ignorance, as Keynes put it, hang over every investment decision. Indeed, they hang over society as a whole. Yet societies create institutions to try to withstand and offset time and ignorance. The list includes social welfare and insurance systems; healthcare; national education; defence, police, and emergency services; and institutions to uphold the rule of law. These are also "investments": long-term institutions created, not usually for profit, but to provide real solutions to problems encountered. The financing of such "investments" has to be regular, irrespective of economic fortunes. If there is a severe downturn, disturbing the flow of public finance to maintain even institutions like these, it is as if doubt and fear infect the very structures of society.

It was grasped in nineteenth-century London that a central bank would have to stand ready to dampen unreasoning panics between banks in the money market, which could otherwise cause all trade credit—and the commercial life of the country—to freeze. The counter-intuitive doctrine that in a financial panic, when all banks refuse to lend, the Bank of England should lend funds freely to other banks, at a high rate of interest and against good collateral, was set out by Walter Bagehot (1826–1877) after the collapse of a major UK bank in 1866; and dusted off again over a century later after the next collapse of a major UK bank in 2007, when

Northern Rock went down in the global financial crisis. A health care system for banks in a panic ("a panic, in a word, is a species of neuralgia, and according to the rules of science you must not starve it", as Bagehot put it in *Lombard Street*) existed long before the creation of a welfare state for human beings.

## Two Views of the Past

There is, of course, a crucially important political backdrop to Hayek's description in 1945, at the end of the Second World War, of a decentralised economy. The Second World War was, as Churchill said, the "unnecessary war", flowing from policy failures after the end of the First World War, just over twenty years before. These included the failure to maintain collective security, stop rearmament by Germany and uphold the will of the League of Nations.

There were grave economic failings too. In *The Economic Consequences of the Peace*, published in 1919 at the conclusion of the First World War, Keynes, present as a UK Treasury official at the Versailles peace conference, denounced the vengeful peace terms and imposition of unpayable reparations on Germany, and the complete absence of any overall plan or scheme to rebuild a prosperous European economy. Keynes was ignored: European reconstruction did not take place. Ten years later, in 1929, Wall Street crashed. A credit-induced bubble in the stocks of US companies, growing since 1927, collapsed, taking with it the market value of the companies, much of the nation's savings and the entire US system of credit. Unemployment started to rise, factories to close down, and as the 1930s began the United States entered the Great Depression. In 1930 the US imposed protective tariffs on trade, prompting countermeasures by other countries and the collapse of world commodities and farm prices.

The European economies, still fragile after the First World War, were knocked back down again by the Wall Street crash. In 1931 the major commercial bank Kredit Anstalt failed, to be followed by the collapse of the German banking system. The UK went off the gold standard. The French government repudiated wartime debts to the United States. In Italy, the Fascist alliance, which began in the 1920s, consolidated its grip on the political system. In 1933, in the worst of the Great Depression, banks across the US closed for business. Within a few weeks of each other in 1933 Roosevelt became President of the United States and Hitler became Chancellor of Germany. The first offered hope, and said that "the only thing we have to fear is fear itself". The second offered fear, revenge, and retribution, paving the way to the outbreak of the Second World War a few years later. The whole period from the outbreak of the First World War to the conclusion of the Second World War was seen by many as one long disaster—another "Thirty Years War", as Churchill later put it in *The Second World War*.

So when the attention of western policymakers turned to the reconstruction of the post-war world, avoiding repeating the mistakes of the previous thirty years was the obvious priority. The Bretton Woods agreements of 1944 aimed at creating global rules to stabilise international money and finance, with currencies linked to the dollar and the dollar linked to gold. The Marshall Plan, the Organisation for European Economic Cooperation and the institutions of what became the European Union were to stop a second post-war slump and a repeat of the revenge cycles of the inter-war years all over again. The 1947 General Agreement on Tariffs and Trade (which became the World Trade Organisation) was to stop a repeat of protectionist trade wars.

On the eastern side of Europe, the conclusions were, however, somewhat different. The centrally planned state-run economies of Europe after the Second World War—and before that the Communist system of the Soviet Union, created after the Russian revolution of 1917—emerged from a different reading of history. The centrally planned economies of the Communist world were not actually foreseen by Marx, but the Marxist theory on which they were based derived from his observations of the failings of the capitalist economy in an earlier phase, that of the nineteenth century. The two parts of Europe became out of step with each other: the lessons of the nineteenth-century informed the thinking of the east; the lessons of the twentieth century the thinking of the west.

Karl Marx (1818–1883) spent much of his life in London and devoted himself to trying to understand the meaning of the revolutionary changes sweeping through the most advanced of European societies: political change since the French revolution; the scientific revolution; and the industrial revolution, with the application of machines to methods of production. Marx witnessed for himself real crises of nineteenth-century capitalism and went on to provide a theory which explained them, and their inevitability. In the Marxist analysis, the flaw in the system lies within economic production itself. The capitalist producer—the owner of a factory—has no choice but to compete with other capitalist producers, and in so doing is forced to invest in ever more expensive machinery, reducing the rate of profit. The capitalist crisis comes—and recurs—because producers invest in machinery to the point where they overproduce, they have no more profit, workers are made unemployed, output is dumped on the market, prices and wages collapse and the cycle begins again, each time on a larger scale than the last.

By locating the flaw in the capitalist system in the method of production, Marxist theory pointed the way to an obvious resolution of its crises: the state should control the means of production, not leave it to the vagaries of the market, and the capitalists. Marx of course did not witness the Wall Street crash of 1929 or the global financial crisis of 2008, but, since he believed that capitalism was fated to move from crisis to crisis, would not have been surprised by either. And yet, state control of the means of production, when it was actually tried in the Soviet Union and in the countries of the CMEA after the Second World War, proved not to be the right answer either. Havel's epitaph on the centrally planned economy, above, still stands.

A subtly different answer to the crises of capitalism was offered by Keynes in the 1930s, after the Wall Street crash, and the Great Depression. To do this, Keynes introduced the technical concept of the "marginal efficiency of capital". This is less fearsome than it sounds. For any given new capital asset (like a new factory), Keynes reasoned, there are two important variables. One is the price of that asset (or what is sometimes called its replacement cost). This is a current price. The second is the prospective yield of that asset, throughout its whole lifetime, possibly of many years. The yield is the return to the owner from selling its output, after deducting the running expenses of obtaining that output. This is not a current price, but a current *expectation*. The marginal efficiency of capital is the point where the prospective yield of a capital asset, discounted to the present day, is equal to its current price.

Equipped with this concept, Keynes can then explain booms and busts, and crises, as fluctuations in the marginal efficiency of capital. How so? Because the second of the two variables, the prospective yield of capital assets, is only based on current expectations, and current expectations can change very suddenly. In a boom, he said, there are optimistic expectations as to the future yield of capital assets, sufficiently strong to offset their growing abundance and their rising costs of production and, probably, a rise in the interest rate. So long as the boom continues much new investment shows a reasonable current yield. Problems start to arise when doubts creep in about the reliability of prospective yield, perhaps because it shows signs of falling off, as the stock of newly produced durable goods steadily increases.

Keynes then brings a further factor into the picture, which is the role of financial markets. Because "speculation" can overwhelm "enterprise" (see above), stock prices can easily part company from any reasonable estimate of long-term yield, as in the credit-induced bubble in stocks of US companies before the Wall Street crash in 1929. And when disillusion comes to fall upon an over-optimistic and overbought investment market, it falls with "sudden and even catastrophic force". This creates a collapse in the marginal efficiency of capital, precipitating a bust, or, as in the 1930s, the Great Depression, when new investment in the US ground to a complete halt.

Keynes therefore provides the missing link between capital investment, economic crises, and financial markets. Although actual investment is carried out by businesses, not by private investors in the financial markets, it is almost impossible for businesses to ignore their own stock market price. Yet market estimates of the marginal efficiency of capital go through enormously wide fluctuations, which lead to fluctuations in levels of economic activity, and (as in the 1930s) fluctuations in employment.

So Keynes ends up in a different place from Marx. For Marx, the capitalist crisis is a crisis of production; for Keynes it is a crisis of investment. For twentieth century followers of Marx the answer became state control of the means of production. For Keynes, unless there is a far-reaching change in the psychology of investment markets (which he thought unlikely), the conclusion is, instead, that "the duty of ordering the current volume of investment cannot safely be left in private hands". It is not the means of production the state needs to get involved in at all: it is ensuring there is a steady flow of investment. By some method or another (he was agnostic as to which), the state has to correct or offset wild fluctuations in the marginal efficiency of capital caused by the fact that investment markets are prone to over-optimism, doubt, fear and panic attacks. This was the message of *The General Theory of Employment, Interest and Money*.

## The End of History

The collapse of the Marx-inspired Communist system in Europe towards the end of the twentieth century presented a real conundrum to policymakers. Apart from it being almost completely unexpected, no-one knew exactly what to do in response. As the President of the European Bank for Reconstruction and Development, set up to try to deal with it, put it, many people had written books explaining how to turn a capitalist economy socialist: no-one on how to reverse the process. It was obvious that the planned economy of the CMEA had failed; but how to undo planning and create a decentralised economy, while minimising the damage of transition between the two?

The writer was, for a while, connected with the European Bank for Reconstruction and Development, as speechwriter for the President (penning a speech on the line from James Joyce, "history is a nightmare from which I am trying to awake", published worldwide), and might here offer some personal remarks.

The collapse of Communism was a moment of huge significance for Europe and the wider world, and yet no-one rose to the occasion. Unlike after the end of the Second World War, when new international political and economic structures were created, there was no over-arching strategy or design. More, perhaps, like after the end of the First World War, the "victors" of the cold war were unable to work out exactly what to do with their victory. Post-Communist Europe had to accommodate itself to the existing European system, in a piece-meal way, as best it could.

Of the states party to the Soviet bloc through the CMEA, one (the GDR) disappeared; one (Czechoslovakia) later split in two; and the largest (the USSR) fragmented into fifteen separate parts. Another (Yugoslavia) fragmented into half a dozen separate parts, several at war with each other. The EU developed a patchwork of economic, political, and trade relations with these formerly Communist states, in 1993 offering the possibility of membership to those fulfilling certain economic and political conditions, including the "capacity to cope with competitive pressure and market forces within the Union". By 2004 eight former-Communist states had joined the EU, along the way importing the vast corpus of EU law, built up in the west since the 1950s. But post-Communist Europe suffered great economic hardships in moving from one system to another. Trade collapsed between former CMEA members; economies shrank; living standards fell. And the grafting process meant in some cases that the roots of democracy were shallow.

The absence of a strategy may well have had a deeper cause, in that the accommodation of centrally planned economies to western European "competitive pressure and market forces" appeared to many to be a simple inevitability, as it was crystal clear that the old Marxist dogmas were defunct. Complacency replaced strategy.

A warning that all was not well in the capitalist world might, however, have been detected as early as 1990, only a year after the fall of the Berlin Wall. In that year there came the unexpected collapse of the Tokyo stock market and the Japanese property-based credit bubble, built up during the 1980s, when property prices increased five to six times in the space of a few years. Until that collapse, Japan had been widely admired as one of the world's most advanced and innovative market economies. A long recession ensued after the Tokyo crash, the effects of which were felt in Japan for decades afterwards.

The collapse of Communism itself had an economic explanation which Marx might have appreciated. A consequence of the delinking of the dollar from gold on the suspension of the Bretton Woods system, in 1971, was instability in the dollar-denominated international oil price, which increased massively during the 1970s. This had the side-effect of greatly increasing the volume of dollars held by oil-producing countries, including dollars held in the accounts of large international commercial banks, who then proceeded to recycle their dollar inflows to governments and government-owned firms, mostly in Latin America but also in CMEA countries like Poland, Hungary, and the GDR. These countries thus ran up huge dollar-denominated debts, requiring IMF and World Bank assistance programmes when they ran into debt repayment difficulties. The high international oil price also led the Soviet Union to cut back on subsidised oil transfers to other CMEA countries, putting further pressure on their economies. Communism was undermined, in effect, by the internal contradictions of global capitalism.

Further warning signs came later in the 1990s, with a new credit bubble in South East Asia. The South East Asia financial crisis, which started in Thailand in 1997, led to interlinked financial collapse across the region, and in 1998 the Russian financial system collapsed too, as the crisis spread across emerging economies. The incomplete reforms to the Soviet economy since the ending of Communism were now thrown into turmoil, and Russia defaulted on international debt repayments. Internal Russian living standards and incomes fell dramatically. From 1999, when Vladimir Putin came to power after the crisis (where he has remained ever since), Russia pulled away from the European market system once more. Russia abandoned Communism, but a financial crisis got in the way, and halted

Russia's potential move to the open society. As Marx might have put it, the first Russian revolution ended in tragedy; the second in psychodrama.

## Minsky's Moment

In 1986 an unknown American economist named Hyman Minsky (1919–1996) published a work providing new intellectual tools for understanding the role of finance in the economy, but it was not until after the 2008 global financial crisis that Minsky's views became better known. What Minsky suggested is that there is not one, but *two* price systems in the market economy. There is a price system for the current output of current goods and services, and the need to recover costs; and then there is a second price system for the values placed upon future income flows from outstanding financial and capital assets.

When Minsky published *Stabilizing an Unstable Economy* the growth of the world's huge financial markets had really only just begun. Financial assets in the form of stocks and bonds were well known, but the idea of foreign exchange as a financial asset class for investors took off later in the 1990s. Commodities (including Hayek's own example of tin) became viewed as a financial asset class only in the early 2000s. The expanding world of financial assets entailed the expansion of Minsky's second price system—to a point where it outstripped the first.

So Hayek's telecommunications system, put forward in 1945, turns out to be only part of the picture. The decentralised western market economy, producing the current output of goods and services, may well be able to use price signals to bring dispersed practical knowledge together. But the same cannot be said about income flows from financial and capital assets. Prices in this system are valuing *future* income flows—and that future is always unknown. Prices are not bringing dispersed practical knowledge together, because that knowledge does not exist. Although knowledge could perhaps be created, if a scientific method were followed, expectations based on collective custom, habit, psychology, and story-telling remain dominant. The signals that reach the economy are not of knowledge but signals of doubt, fear, memories of last time and hope that next time will be different and better: a veritable soap opera of sentiment.

Hayek in 1945 was concerned with the best way of building a rational economic order. This order was largely built in the decentralised western market economy, into which Communism subsequently collapsed. But alongside it—and particularly after the end of the constraints on private finance imposed by the Bretton Woods system in the 1970s—a less than rational economic order emerged too. Apparently similar, but actually different, the speculative financial economy came in the end to outgrow the economy of the real world. The implications of this form the subject matter of this book.

So was Havel wrong when he spoke of "living in truth"? Is the idea of truth an impossible standard to uphold, or a demand to make? Theories in the sciences which explain the future must be testable (or "falsifiable", in the term used by the philosopher of knowledge Karl Popper [1902–1994]). What is being tested is a claim that a theory is true—which means that it corresponds to the facts, or that things are as it describes. Although Popper held that all scientific theories and knowledge are provisional, he did not mean that truth does not exist. He thought it does; and it is indispensable to the critical scientific approach.

Living in truth did help Havel and his fellow dissidents see through the errors of the Communist system of the twentieth century. This was a major achievement. In the next chapter we will focus on what happens when, after a major financial crash, as in 2008, the search for truth is abandoned, and we pass through the looking-glass into a post-truth world.

## References


Bagehot W, *Lombard Street: A Description of the Money Market*, 1901, London, Kegan Paul, Trench, Trübner and Co.

Churchill W, "The Iron Curtain", *The Speeches of Winston Churchill*, Cannadine D (Ed.), 1990, London, Penguin Books.

Churchill W, *The Second World War*, Vol I, 1965, London, Cassell and Co.

Havel V, "New Year's Address", *Open Letters, Selected Prose*, 1991, London, Faber and Faber.

Hayek F, "The Use of Knowledge in Society", 1945, *American Economic Review*, XXXV, 4.

Keynes JM, *The General Theory of Employment, Interest and Money*, 1936, London, Macmillan.

Minsky H, *Stabilizing an Unstable Economy*, 1986, 2008, New York, McGraw Hill.

CHAPTER 2

# After the Fall

**Abstract** How the collapse in expectations after a financial crisis, like a fault-line in normality, leads to abnormal political events, as on both sides of the Atlantic after the crash of 2008.

**Keywords** Capital assets · Expectations · Polarisation · Financial crises · Investment

## Dark Forces

The brief decade after the global financial crisis of 2008 produced much that would have been unthinkable in the post-war period. The crisis led not only to steep economic downturns in many developed countries, but shattered confidence in the economic and political competence of incumbent governments and institutions in the democracies on both sides of the Atlantic. In the United States and Europe "elites" and "establishments" came under attack from populist insurgents, representing (or claiming to represent) the disaffected, the dispossessed, and the marginalised. The economic downturn was not as serious as the Great Depression of the 1930s, and the political backlash did not involve a slide to full-blooded totalitarian Fascism, but, all the same, democratic norms were weakened

© The Author(s), under exclusive license to Springer Nature Switzerland AG 2021

D. Harrison, *Capitalism and the Dark Forces of Time and Ignorance*, https://doi.org/10.1007/978-3-030-78394-5_2

and demagogues and autocrats strengthened in ways unimaginable to earlier generations.

All this was contrary to Hayek's bold idea in 1945 that the market system would work to spread useful and practical knowledge around the world, and so help build a rational economic order. How did this breakdown in the post-war norms of accepted behaviour happen?

A major financial crisis like that of 2008 is more than just a recession, or a downturn in the economy. It is like a severe jolt to reality itself. Structures which had seemed secure become uncertain. What was valuable becomes valueless. Assets become liabilities. Profits become losses. Debts mount and good collateral becomes suspect, or worthless.

As described by Keynes in the 1930s, but largely forgotten in the post-war period, a crisis is a sudden shift, or a collapse, in the marginal efficiency of capital, which rests heavily upon precarious expectations of the future. Expectations of long-term yields of capital assets suddenly change, and new investments which looked profitable at one moment look unprofitable the next, so they are not entered into. The result is that the economy draws in its collective breath. Plans remain unexecuted. Stagnation ensues, until expectations of yields improve, which may not happen spontaneously until the entire stock of capital assets is run down—perhaps taking years.

A major crisis, then, is like a rent in the very fabric of society, fully as damaging in economic terms as a physical catastrophe or a war but without any similar visible explanation, in the way an earthquake can be explained, or a fire or flood. It is this invisible character of the dislocation, with causes highly abstract and esoteric, which is perhaps most damaging to social cohesion. As Keynes put it, expectations of the future affect the present through the price of durable equipment. Real, tangible, things—nothing could be more real than durable capital equipment: the buildings, houses, factories, and underpinnings of the modern economy—are mortally affected by unseen forces hardly one person in a million can understand.

The pattern is that during the boom, which precedes the crash, the prices of *existing* capital assets are propelled unsustainably upward, driven not by reason or logic but by collective psychology in investment markets. Much new investment (that is, in new capital assets) takes place during this period. The future is faced with confidence. But in a crash these same prices collapse, with "sudden and even catastrophic force", as in the Wall Street crash of 1929, when secure stocks like General Motors and US

Steel lost 90% and more of their value. The future is faced now with fear. New investment does not take place, slowing the economy to a halt until it can somehow be induced to start again. There are political consequences too: social institutions, structures, and projects built up in the boom are brought down by the crash. So are political leaders: US President Hoover, who came to power in 1929 before the Wall Street crash, became fatally associated with the Depression, about which he could do nothing, and was replaced by Roosevelt in 1933, who tried everything. In 1840 the young Abraham Lincoln nearly abandoned political life after a regional banking crisis caused work he had encouraged on expanding railways, canals, bridges, and roads in Illinois to be brought to an abrupt halt.

A few years later, in the *Communist Manifesto* of 1848, Marx and Engels wrote of the recurring crises of capitalism as if modern bourgeois society had conjured up gigantic means of production and exchange "like the sorcerer, who is no longer able to control the powers of the nether world whom he has called up by his spells". In these commercial crises, threatening the very existence of contemporary society, "a great part not only of the existing products, but also of the previously created productive forces, are periodically destroyed".

A major twist in the cycle of periodic destruction has become the importance to today's economy of capital assets in the shape of property, or real estate. Most bank credit in today's developed world is associated with financing property. The triggering of the 2008 global crisis was a collapse in the market for mortgage-related securities after a fall in real estate prices in the United States. Before the crisis, prices of residential and commercial real estate had increased sharply in developed countries around the world, fuelled by the supply of bank credit. As in the years before the Wall Street crash of 1929, when credit fuelled a bubble in stock prices, credit fuelled a speculative rise in property prices to a point where they became unsustainable, a rickety scaffolding of mortgage-related securities built on them became insecure, and when it fell panic spread through the financial world. The interconnected US and European banking systems, containing enormous volumes of cross-border claims between financial institutions, made the crisis a transatlantic one. The withholding of credit by collapsing banks then hit the prices of property generally, and cut off a source of financing of capital investment by companies, creating a deep recession.

Viewed from the outside, or in retrospect, these processes are, as described here, reasonably comprehensible. There is a rational, if unpalatable, explanation. But viewed from the inside, or as they are happening, by those affected, they hardly seem to make sense at all. Far from spreading knowledge in society, what is going on appears completely irrational—or, worse, caused by someone or something with malign intent, like the nether world powers conjured up by Marx's sorcerer. From this fault-line in normality many abnormal things radiated after 2008.

## The UK Turns Inward

Exhibit A is the sequence of events in the UK, the location of banks collectively five times bigger in 2007 than the national economy, and with London the main European hub of the financial crisis. In the space of a mere ten years after 2008 the UK moved from leading the global response to becoming virtually a pariah state, turning inwards and withdrawing from the post-war cooperative structures of the European Union.

In 2009, in the immediate aftermath of the crisis, the UK government convened a global summit of world leaders in London, which issued the following statement:

> We face the greatest challenge to the world economy in modern times; a crisis which has deepened since we last met, which affects the lives of women, men and children in every country, and which all countries must join together to resolve. A global crisis requires a global solution.

The global coordinated response resulting from the London summit included a major monetary relaxation; a large fiscal boost worth 2% of world GDP over two years; and the biggest guarantee and support for the worldwide banking system yet witnessed, comprising $2 trillion of support and £7 trillion of guarantees.

All this was apposite by way of a crisis response, but in the UK the turn of the domestic electoral cycle then propelled a retreat from international cooperation. In common with other European countries, the incumbent political leadership at the time of the 2008 crisis was evicted from office afterwards, becoming tainted by association with it. After a change of government in 2010 a crisis coalition government was formed which, rather than focusing on promoting global growth and global solutions, focused instead on domestic financial consolidation, and a programme of economic retrenchment.

This policy, prevailing for the remainder of the decade, avoided addressing the global nature of the crisis, concentrating instead on the narrow question of UK public expenditure, and correcting the expansionist policies of the previous government. In the absence of a convincing answer to a difficult question, a different question was addressed.

The result of domestic austerity was virtual economic stagnation, and a decade without any real economic growth. The post-crisis downturn in private economic activity was not offset by increased public activity. It took nearly six years from 2010 for the UK economy to recover its pre-recession level of output. There was not mass unemployment, as in the 1930s, but cutbacks in public expenditure affected many of the most disadvantaged. By 2015 in only two regions in the UK (London and the south east) was real GDP per head back above its pre-crisis peak. In other regions it was still below; in some cases strikingly so. In most regions incomes by 2016 had not experienced a real recovery, except, again, in London, and the south east. So the crisis widened the existing regional distribution of income in the UK, already making the UK one of the most regionally unbalanced countries in the industrialised world, with high levels of economic inequality. Earnings of workers, expressed in real terms, were in 2016 around 5% below the peak in 2009. This was the longest period of flat or falling real wages since the nineteenth century.

A policy of austerity eroded support for the minority crisis coalition partner, who were punished in the UK general election of 2015, and a Conservative party returned with a sufficient majority to govern alone, with a manifesto including, ominously, a commitment to hold an in/out referendum on the question of UK membership of the European Union. The government assumed it would win the referendum when the vote was held in 2016, and the shock caused by the 52/48 victory of the leave vote caused another political leader to be evicted from office and plunged the UK into an unparalleled political, diplomatic and constitutional crisis, dominating the remainder of the decade.

After the referendum it was noticed that capital assets in the shape of property had played their part. Those regions of the country with the smallest increases in property prices voted to leave the EU, as did the twenty-seven areas where property prices declined from 2004 to 2016. Prices of houses doubled between 2004 and 2016 in London, which voted to remain, while they scarcely moved in Hartlepool, which voted to leave, and where comparable property cost about 15% of that in London. Northern Rock, the first major UK bank to collapse since the nineteenth century, had specialised in mortgage finance for property in the north east of England, and house values in that region suffered as a result.

So the decade from 2008 to 2018, when terms of its withdrawal were agreed with the European Union, saw the UK move from a financial crisis to a wider crisis of its entire political and economic system, and what seemed incredible become possible.

## As Does the United States

In the United States, the epicentre of the 2008 global crisis, the decade was also one of political shock. The United States had a relatively good crisis compared to the UK and the rest of Europe, helped by the public injection of funds into the economy via the American Recovery and Reinvestment Act of 2009, and swift action to stabilise US banks, but it nonetheless served to undermine political norms, and boost protectionism.

For some decades before the crisis the US economy had been a study in the perverse effects of financial capitalism. In his monumental *Competitive Advantage of Nations*, first published in 1989, business strategist Michael Porter criticised the financial system developed in the United States since the 1970s for failing American industry. In particular, the rise and method of operation of investment funds (like pension funds), pooling private savings, had come to have a perversely injurious effect on corporate health. Rather than channel savings into long-term investments in industry, and improve the competitiveness of corporations and the US economy, fund management became focused on short-term company share price appreciation. This in turn diverted companies from long-term objectives, such as investing to maintain their market position, stay competitive and grow internationally. Of the ten leading industrial nations Porter studied in preparing his work, American companies were found to have the highest rate of return targets, used to screen new investment opportunities.

"Money manager capitalism" , as the economist Hyman Minsky named it in 1996, had thus already been undermining American industry for decades before the financial crisis of 2008. The financial services industry grew strongly during this same period, including by devising the impossibly complicated mortgage-backed products whose collapse triggered the crisis.

Bailing out the financial system after 2008, and injecting public funds into the failing economy to prevent a severe recession from turning into a depression, were necessary but highly unpopular and controversial in the United States. Unlike in the 1930s, when Roosevelt was able to pin blame for the Great Depression squarely on the "money changers" who in the midst of the crisis had "fled from their high seats in the temple of our civilization", and to devise a series of experimental New Deal policies and banking reforms matching the gravity of the situation, the abstract causes of the crash of 2008 were imperfectly explained, and the lessons to be learned unclear, and in any event widely contested.

The economic recession, the sense (as in the UK) that justice had not been visited on those responsible, the strains on the US budget and the long-term diminishing of good job prospects for many ordinary workers combined to polarise American political discourse. Eight years after a financial crisis rooted in the speculative financing of real estate, the American electorate turned, ironically, to another property speculator in their search for new leadership, in the shape of Donald Trump. In his inaugural address in 2017 Trump spoke of "American carnage", and by the end of the decade following the financial crisis had denounced international cooperation; promoted a unilateral America First foreign policy last seen in the 1930s; and embarked on a series of trade wars with the rest of the world. Trump's first policy adviser, Steve Bannon, traced a direct line between the financial crisis of 2008 and the rise of Trump. As in the UK, the United States saw ten years of retreat from the idea that there was a global crisis requiring a global solution.

## Europe Has No Seatbelts

The unlucky countries hosting the world's two most advanced financial centres, situated on opposite sides of the Atlantic in New York and London, suffered perhaps the greatest political upheavals in the decade after the crisis. But other parts of Europe were not immune. In the case of Greece, the withdrawal of global credit in the aftermath of the crisis revealed an enormous public sector deficit in 2009, many times greater than the level permitted for Greece to join the euro, at its launch in 1999. Trust in the probity of the Greek state evaporated when it emerged that the deficit had been artificially lowered, and statistics submitted by Athens for years to the EU statistics agency could not be relied on. The Greek debt crisis ran on for the remainder of the decade.

Elsewhere in Europe, economies which had boomed on an inflow of credit into property and construction crashed when after the crisis the supply of cheap credit dried up. Thus, in the period 1999–2007 private banking sector debt in Italy had risen by 71%, in Spain by 75%, in Portugal by 49%, and in Ireland by 101%. After the 2008 crisis all these countries went into a severe recession, complicated by the poor state of the banking industry in each; the risks weighing on national public finances of bailing out large and important banks; the scale of debts accumulated; and the fears of contagion from one country to the next.

From 2009 until 2012 it appeared as if the euro itself was under threat, and, as the German chancellor Angela Merkel said in 2011, "if the euro fails, Europe fails". The euro did not fail, thanks very largely to decisive action by the European Central Bank, but a decade after the crisis unemployment was still high in countries most affected; growth was mediocre; and anti-establishment and anti-system political parties, frequently nationalistic and anti-EU in tone, had mushroomed everywhere, including in countries like France and Germany most associated with launch of the euro. No other member state followed the UK down the path of actually trying to leave the EU, but the tensions between the central laws and rules of the EU and the countries within it were palpable. Europe might not actually have failed, but it did not seem to be succeeding either.

An abiding impression of those dealing with the euro-zone crisis at its height was the sheer difficulty of working out what on earth was going on. In the words of the President of the European Council (the institutional meeting of heads of state and government), looking back on events in *Europe in the Storm*, "We were entering into stormy weather. 'Fasten your seatbelts' was the motto—except for the fact that no seatbelts had been foreseen by our predecessors. We had to build a lifeboat in the middle of the storm". If the elected leaders of some of the most mature democracies in the world had difficulty understanding what was happening, their electorates cannot be blamed for feeling lost too.

## The Lure of the Far-Right

So on both sides of the Atlantic, in the United States and Europe, the decade after the crisis was something of a lost decade, with a turning inward almost everywhere, a putting up of barriers (mental, spiritual, political and in some cases physical) and an invocation of ancient mystical notions of "sovereignty" instead of the straightforward idea in 2009 that a global crisis requires a global solution.

That a financial crisis takes about a decade for its effects to work through may be a rule of thumb: there was a similar "lost decade" in Latin America in the 1980s after a sudden stop in the flow of inward commercial credit in 1982, and the resulting debt crisis. After the Wall Street crash of 1929, Keynes, noting the collapse in aggregate net investment in the United States in the period from 1925 to 1933, postulated that two main factors affect the duration of a slump. First, new investment does not begin until there is a rise in the marginal efficiency of capital, which in turn is linked to the length of life of existing capital assets, and when they become scarce through use, decay or obsolescence. Secondly, the impact of carrying-over of surplus stocks, built up during the preceding boom, has to work its way through too: disposing of these surpluses, with their own rising carrying-costs, typically takes several years. Absorbing these stocks is like negative investment: it is a deterrent to employment.

In 2016 three German academics published a paper looking at the effect on democratic politics of financial crises since 1870, covering twenty advanced countries, and more than 800 general elections. From "Going to Extremes: Politics after Financial Crises, 1870–2014" it is evident that what happened in Europe and the United States in the decade since 2008 is not unusual. After a financial crisis it is common for policy uncertainty and polarisation to rise. After a crisis, voters seem to be particularly attracted to the political rhetoric of the extreme right, which often attributes blame to minorities or foreigners: on average extreme right-wing parties increase their vote share by 30%. The evidence assembled by Funke, Schularick, and Trebesche is of financial crises putting great strains on modern democracies: votes for far-right parties increasing; government majorities shrinking; the fractionalisation of parliaments rising; and the number of parties represented jumping.

Before the war striking examples can be found in Italy and Germany. Mussolini's Fascist alliance benefited electorally from the early 1920s banking crisis in Italy and the global recession after the end of the First

World War; Nazi electoral support in Germany peaked in 1933, with the Great Depression at its strongest in Central Europe.

After the 2008 global crisis far-right and right-wing populist parties more than doubled their vote share in many advanced countries, including France, the UK, Sweden, Finland, the Netherlands, Portugal, and Japan. Similar effects were observed after purely regional financial crises, such as the Scandinavian banking crisis of the late 1980s and early 1990s. (And although Russia fell outside the scope of the 2016 study, Vladimir Putin became President soon after the collapse of the Russian financial system in 1998, starting a career as leader seemingly without end.)

"Going to Extremes" suggests that about ten years after a financial crisis politics may return to normal; far-right votes diminish, as does political radicalisation and the fractionalisation of parliaments. This may be reassuring; but, on the other hand, countries which have gone too far do not turn back: pre-war Germany and Italy are examples; and, possibly, modern Russia. The jury is out on the UK, as it cuts itself off from the EU's cooperative legal system.

## This Time Is Not Different

Financial crises are aberrations of industrial, capitalist societies, and, as is abundantly evident, create enormous strains on the societies they affect. What is striking is not how rare they are but how common. According to the tally compiled by American economists Reinhart and Rogoff in *This Time Is Different* (2009) there have been, in total, 40 banking crises since 1800 in the world's top financial centres, situated in the USA, the UK, and France. Crises of industrial capital in the nineteenth century prompted Marx, and later Communist leaders and states, to promote revolution and state control of the economy as the remedy. Crises in the twentieth century have opened the way more to the far-right, who have in most cases sought scapegoats and blamed minorities, foreigners, or governing elites as a route to gaining power. Whether these extremist tendencies can be reversed seems to depend largely on the severity of the crisis and the robustness of the political system under attack—and perhaps also on sheer luck.

The paradox is that industrial capitalism nurtures democracy and thrives under it, but also erupts in periodic crises which threaten to destroy it. These crises may have disastrous consequences and yet, below the surface, the process is explicable enough. Industrial capitalism requires investment if it is to function, but investment is a process vulnerable to the behaviour of investment markets, more driven by speculation than making reasonable estimates of yields. Views of the future, determining whether new investment takes place, are volatile and unsteady, and prone to collective excesses of self-reinforcing optimism (in a boom), and pessimism (in a crash).

Keynes's observations in the *General Theory* were based on the Wall Street crash of 1929 and the Great Depression, and he put twentieth-century crises together with nineteenth-century trade cycles. Some updating is needed to account for more modern financial crises. In the United States, for example, account needs to be taken of "money manager capitalism", and the way in which since the late twentieth century most financial management is carried out by professional investment funds, focused on the share price appreciation of the companies they invest in.

The largest booms and busts in financial crises of recent decades have been associated with property, but the Keynesian analysis can be brought up to date without too much difficulty. Property, in particular commercial property, is a capital asset like any other, and dangers arise when property prices part company from underlying yields, represented usually by the commercial rents obtainable. Excessive bank credit into commercial property can cause prices to rise unsustainably above historic rent levels, until (as invariably happens) the flow of credit slows, or is curtailed, and prices tumble, leaving debts behind, based on the over-optimistic pre-crash prices.

A large part of all modern bank credit goes into property, and the rising and falling of property prices determine the fortunes of banks. Across the developed world, the average share of bank credit devoted to the financing, or refinancing, of property is estimated to have risen from about 35% in 1970 to a figure approaching 60% by 2007. In the UK 65% of all bank lending was devoted to residential mortgages by 2012, and a further 14% to commercial real estate (so making 79% in total).

Domestic or residential property can be thought of in a similar way to commercial property, even if the owner is not renting it out. The "yield" to the owner is the value of living in a property over the long term, after deducting running costs. Where credit (mortgages from banks) becomes easy the price of such property becomes an object in itself, and speculative appreciation in price takes over from "yield". Buying and selling houses becomes more important than living in them. When, as happened in the United States, credit-induced price appreciation reaches its limits and prices tumble, those with high proportions of credit to the value of properties become indebted. In the United States, between 2007 and 2016, an estimated nearly 10 million mortgage borrowers lost their homes.

Although financial crises are associated with modern industrial capitalism, Keynes thought similar economic effects could be traced back to old pre-industrial days. Before the industrial revolution, societies based on agriculture also suffered large-scale economic fluctuations, but these depended on whether there were good or bad harvests. Keynes suggested in the *General Theory* that after a very good harvest there is usually an important addition to the normal carry-over of stocks to later years, and this addition is the same in economic terms as an increase in current investment. Conversely, after a very poor harvest the carry-over to later years is consumed, and this is the same as a reduction in investment. In a society where agriculture is the predominant industry, fluctuations in investment arrived at in these ways could be extremely large—perhaps only surpassed in their effects by war.

## Scapegoats Must Be Found

Although in 1945 Hayek saw the price system leading to the better use of knowledge in post-war society, the decade since the 2008 global financial crisis has seen knowledge and problem-solving beat a retreat. In the UK, within a few short years, the language of elected heads of government shifted from saying (in 2009) that a global crisis requires a global solution, to saying (in 2016) that "if you believe you're a citizen of the world, you're a citizen of nowhere. You don't understand what the very word 'citizenship' means". Plus, "too many people in positions of power" behave as though they have more in common with "international elites" than "the people down the road".

The United States, too, signed up to the 2009 London crisis summit statement. But by 2018 the US President had espoused an America First isolationism; denounced global cooperation; withdrawn from international agreements on matters like climate change and trade; and embarked on an economic policy based on elevating protectionist tariffs and conducting trade wars. As Trump put it in a speech in 2017: "Our government rushed to join international agreements where the United States pays the costs and bears the burdens, while other countries get the benefit and pay nothing".

That political leaders of the most highly advanced capitalist economies depict their electorates as victims suffering at the hands of unnamed others ("international elites"; "other countries") indicates they have lost control of events. In a similar fashion, after the Wall Street crash of 1929, US President Hoover signed into law in 1930 a protectionist trade tariff (Smoot-Hawley), despite the entreaties of a thousand economists not to do so, and the wholly predictable retaliatory tariffs imposed by the rest of the world, which then led to the destruction of the world trading community, so making the US Depression worse.

Other developed countries did not embark on trade wars and isolationism after the 2008 financial crisis to the same degree as the United States and the UK (via "Brexit"), but the theme of blaming international elites, institutions and rules became a common one. In France, Germany, Italy, Hungary, and Poland (in particular) far-right and anti-establishment and nationalist parties grew in power and strength, blaming (variously) the European Union; immigrants; international financiers (George Soros); predecessor political parties; and the mainstream media.

It was, of course, as nothing compared to the complete renunciation of reason and cooperation in Europe in the inter-war period of the 1930s. Mussolini's Fascists embarked on a policy of war and living dangerously; Hitler's Nazis saw barbarism as an honourable title, and pursued domestic traitors (who settled the terms of peace after the First World War); Jews; cosmopolitan bankers; and intellectuals. Other forms of Fascism sprang up in other European countries during the same Depression.

It appears that financial crises, and the economic turmoil following, serve to narrow the horizons of what is politically possible. Just as Keynes's marginal efficiency of capital rests upon expectations of the future which suddenly collapse, so the political future itself collapses too and the near term becomes more important than the long term. The immediate locality and tribe become more important, and perhaps even appear more real, than distant neighbours, or the safety of the world itself.

Unfortunately, this foreshortening effect is exactly the opposite of what is needed to combat a large-scale financial crisis. Expectations of the future need to be held steady over the longer term to allow investment to resume, and the crisis to heal itself. International cooperation needs to increase, not diminish, if the global nature of a crisis is to be addressed. A banking panic is, as Bagehot put it, like a disease of the nerves, "a species of neuralgia"—and according to the rules of science the treatment is not a starvation diet.

In his famous nineteenth-century work of anthropology *The Golden Bough*, James George Frazer suggested that many religions originally sprang from fertility cults revolving around the worship and periodic sacrifice of a sacred king, the incarnation of a dying and reviving god—who died at the harvest and was reincarnated in the spring. If we put this beside Keynes's suggestion that massive economic fluctuations in old agricultural societies were linked to very good, or very poor, harvests and the carry-over of stocks, we might conjecture that the pursuit of modern scapegoats, after financial crises, is simply a modern re-enactment of patterns of human behaviour found in myths and legends whose economic origins go back through all of humanity, since agriculture became the basis of civilisation.

The "marvel" of Hayek's price system, bringing real dispersed knowledge together, turns out to be a fragile construction, capable of being overturned by economic disaster. Nonetheless, modern industrial capitalism, dating from the industrial revolution onwards, does still rest squarely upon the development of knowledge, and the displacement of old myths and legends, or pre-scientific explanations of phenomena, by robust scientific theories. Capital assets themselves—buildings, factories, telecommunications grids, transport systems—anything giving a yield of income—can only exist in the first place through the development of scientific knowledge. It is the *crises* of industrial capitalism, and their effects on the many millions of people who suffer from them, which cause the reactions threatening to take societies backwards to tribal, pre-industrial and pre-scientific times. In the next chapter we will look a little more into the conditions permitting such events to happen.

## References

Frazer JG, *The Golden Bough: A Study in Comparative Religion*, 1890, London, Macmillan.

Funke M, Schularick M and Trebesche C, "Going to Extremes: Politics After Financial Crises, 1870–2014", *European Economic Review*, 2016, 88, C.

Marx K and Engels F, "The Communist Manifesto", *Karl Marx: A Reader*, Elster J (Ed.), 1989, Cambridge, Cambridge University Press.

Minsky H, "Uncertainty and the Institutional Structure of Capitalist Economies", 1996, Working Paper No. 155, Jerome Levy Economics Institute of Bard College.

Porter M, *The Competitive Advantage of Nations*, 1990, 1998, Basingstoke, Palgrave.
Reinhart C and Rogoff K, *This Time Is Different*, 2009, Princeton, Princeton University Press.
Van Rompuy H, *Europe in the Storm*, 2014, Leuven, Davidsfonds Uitgeverij.

CHAPTER 3

# The Medium Is (Still) the Message

**Abstract** How the speculative approach of attempting to forecast the psychology of the market has influenced the worlds of media and politics.

**Keywords** Psychology of the market · Narrative economics · Narrative politics · Globalisation

## Inside Knowledge

How did conditions emerge in recent decades so that an essentially narrow and technical question—a sudden shift, or collapse, in the marginal efficiency of capital—might expand to become a general crisis of the western economic model; and the worst crisis of the democratic world since 1945?

Both the creation and use of knowledge and the difficulty of predicting the future have had an impact on modern industrial society, on both sides of the Atlantic. On the one hand, the incremental growth and development of the capitalist economic system since the industrial revolution has relied heavily upon the scientific method. This method is one of trial and error, of testing and falsifying scientific theories permitting the development of industrial processes and technology. Aircraft fly, buildings and bridges stay upright and medicines cure diseases because behind them are

© The Author(s), under exclusive license to Springer Nature Switzerland AG 2021

D. Harrison, *Capitalism and the Dark Forces of Time and Ignorance*, https://doi.org/10.1007/978-3-030-78394-5_3

robust theories tested in endless experiments, with effects reproducible at will by anyone with the right level of knowledge and expertise.

The development of modern machinery played an important role in Marx's own nineteenth-century investigation into capitalism. In *A World to Win* (2018), an exhaustive account of his life and works, Liedman explains how Marx took care in *Capital* to define a machine quite precisely, as needing to have three parts: a motor mechanism, to create movement; a transmitting mechanism, to convey, regulate or convert movement by means such as drive shafts and gears; and a tool or working part, to turn movement into tasks. Hayek in 1945 used the image of a telecommunications system to describe the price-signalling mechanism in a decentralised economy: an up to date piece of high quality, state of the art, technology.

There is nothing speculative about such machines or such technology. The bedrock is, on the contrary, one of critical rationalism. Capital assets—providing a stream of income over a long period of time—rest upon proven technology, which in turn depends upon a scientific, critical, approach. No modern capital asset—factory, productive process, office block, patent-protected invention, communications system, or transport network—could exist or work or produce a stream of income for its owner over a period of years without a scientific rationale of some kind behind it. The phenomenon of globalisation itself relies upon networks of such capital assets.

On the other hand, the *financing* of new capital assets—or investment—is subject to the play of powerful speculative forces. Lacking a stable basis for assessing an uncertain future, collective opinion in investment markets, or what Keynes called a "conventional" market valuation, predominates. Rather than calculating streams of income from capital assets—the likely return from selling their output, after running expenses, when machines, systems and technology are put to work—a conventional basis is what investment markets currently and collectively expect the future to be. When this conventional basis of expectations becomes over-optimistic and then collapses back, so does investment and so does the economy, since the economy needs a steady stream of new investment to keep going.

It is worth pausing here over speculation, in the sense that Keynes meant it. This is the activity of attempting to forecast "the psychology of the market". It is different in kind from attempting to forecast a real-world event, such as whether a capital asset will work technically as it should. Speculation involves participants in financial markets aiming to guess, sooner than anyone else, the way the market itself—composed of all the other participants in the market—will go. Another expression Keynes used in the *General Theory* is of speculators having the object of securing profit "from knowing better than the market what the future will bring forth".

The market here is not some impersonal, abstract entity, or the mathematical construct of economists, but a composition of countless individuals, each attempting to work out what everyone else is doing and thinking. Real, fixed, values do not matter so much as what everyone else thinks those values will be. In the real world a yard will be a yard, and a metre will be a metre, but in speculative markets if enough people think a metre is worth two metres that is what it will be—to enough people.

Keynes emphasised the psychological influences over such investment markets, susceptible to unreasoning waves of emotion, or triggered by irrelevant impulse. Expectations shift and change restlessly, seeking to fix on an organising principle or narrative to give direction. Plausible—but untested—beliefs, stories, and factoids shape majority opinion. In the *General Theory* he cited the phenomenon of higher prices for stocks of American ice manufacturers in the summer than in winter; and the market valuation of the entire British railway system going up because of the recurrence of a bank holiday.

More recent examples of plausible, widely shared, and yet incorrect, beliefs include notions like "countries don't go bankrupt" (and therefore US bank lending in the 1970s to state and state-backed businesses in developing countries was completely safe); "information technology changes everything" (and therefore rocketing IT stock prices in the 1990s were fully justified); and "property prices never fall" (and therefore securely propped up a twenty-first-century pyramid of complex securities built on top). Unlike the rigorous testing by trial and error involved in designing and creating capital assets, what the US economist Robert Shiller has called "narrative economics" propagates, develops and multiplies—until a plausible narrative runs into reality itself.

Speculation, even if driven by emotion rather than critical rationalism, is a powerful force. Isaac Newton himself got his fingers burnt in a financial bubble in the eighteenth century—the South Sea Company bubble, promising a lucrative monopoly of British trade with South America. Subdued in the immediate post-war period, it has grown as finance has grown in the decades after the ending of the Bretton Woods system.

Countervailing pressures have weakened: the rules stabilising exchange rates largely abandoned; limits on the creation of credit by banks lifted; and fixed commission rates on trading in stocks abolished, in the largest US and UK stock markets. By the twenty-first century volumes of transactions in foreign exchange markets had thus become over 70 times greater than actual global trade. Stock trading in the United States, with an average annual volume of $33 trillion, had become over 100 times greater than the $250 billion of new capital brought annually to US companies by issuing shares. And property price bubbles, supported by bank credit, had formulated themselves in hotspots virtually everywhere around the world.

Within the financial sector, the explosion in volumes of activity, increased volatility (and the creation of new financial instruments to try to contain it), low fixed costs and high, but variable, costs of staff remuneration, combined to make profits extremely high. By 2007 (the year before the global crash of 2008) finance was estimated to account for 40% of aggregate corporate profits in the United States and the UK.

Firms in this sector appeared to be at the heart of the global economy. As depicted by Philip Augar, a former investment banker, in *The Greed Merchants*, published just before the crisis of 2008, the largest Wall Street investment banks had become like giant stock exchanges, with global reach and multi-product inventories. They had better knowledge than any other institution or organisation in the world about the world's economy—they knew more than their clients and their smaller competitors; more than central banks and national legislatures; and more than the Secretary of the US Treasury and the Chancellor of the UK Exchequer.

The knowledge flowing through these giant stock exchanges was, in particular, knowledge of transactions in the financial sector itself. Knowledge of what was happening or about to happen ahead of the rest of the market was a priceless advantage. The larger the institution, the more information about the state of the market to be derived from interactions with other participants. That gave it its edge. And it gave a collective edge to the largest participants, grouped together under the heading "Wall Street". In such a way, forecasting "the psychology of the market" had become, to a significant degree, a matter of looking in the mirror.

## Artists of the Floating World

The use of knowledge has clashed with the conventions of society in other ways.

After the end of Bretton Woods the media followed finance. The soap opera sentiments of doubt and fear to be found in speculative markets, and the power of folk memory of the past over knowledge of the future, are admirably suited to modern mass communications, capable of transmitting and amplifying signals of emotion, irrespective of the truth, or otherwise, of their content. Exciting stories and narratives nearly always sell more media space than sober accounts of pure scientific rationality.

Modern mass communications and digital platforms depend, it is true, upon highly advanced technology and sophisticated and expensive capital assets, resting upon a scientific, rational, approach, if they are to function at all. But that does not mean that the content has to be scientific or rational. The streams of income from the costly capital assets which are digital and media platforms depend on high volumes of use. The modern model of social media with free content for the user relies upon generating advertising revenue somehow, and the more attention-seeking narratives and stories earn higher revenues.

The mass media—newspapers, journals, pamphlets, television, books, cinema, all the precursors of today's mass electronic and social media platforms—have, of course, always included a large entertainment element, only loosely connected to the facts. In Hermann Hesse's classic novel *The Glass Bead Game*, the twenty-third-century inhabitants of a future civilisation look back regretfully on the late nineteenth century, and the period before the First World War, as the "Age of the Feuilleton" (a supplement to a newspaper devoted to sensationalist gossip and features). Particularly popular were interviews with well known personalities on current events: chemists and musicians giving their views on politics; and dancers, gymnasts, aviators, and poets giving their views on the causes of financial crises. The simple trick was to couple a well known name with a well known subject.

With speculation playing such a large role in the modern economy, and those involved in it seeming so very profitable, the erratic signals emanating from the world of finance have been vested with immense media significance. Reporting of 24-hour global financial market developments has given a mounting and exciting sense of time speeding up—as, ironically, the underlying economies have been slowing down. A story can always be had about stocks, or currencies, or commodities, whether they are going up or down. Connected stories about who or which firm is doing well, or poorly, or who thinks the market will move in one direction or another, generate media content too.

Vast fortunes have been built on the huge volumes of data produced and consumed by financial markets. The wealthiest candidate in the 2020 US Presidential race, Michael Bloomberg, with a publicly reported personal wealth of $55.5 billion, owed it to the software and specialist terminals provided by his firm to financial institutions around the world since the 1980s, allowing them to transact with one another, and exchange information.

There is, inevitably, then a close connection between the worlds of media and politics. Political leaders need access to the media to communicate with the general public; and media owners, and journalists, need access to political leaders to create content. Political leaders have specialist media advisers with communications skills; and members of the media become prized advisers to politicians and governments.

Much political journalism is, however, strikingly similar to speculation, in the sense of the word used for investment markets—the essence is to forecast the shifting psychology of public opinion, and ideally to shape it too. Rather similar too is the concentration on the short term, and extrapolating into the far future the consequences of immediate events.

And although global communications allow real knowledge to be distributed around the world, it is not easy to locate in the high volume of noise. This is by contrast with Hayek's price-signalling system, where prices transmit the minimum of practical knowledge of changing events to those who need it. Genuine scientific knowledge may be shared more easily through communications technology within the scientific community; and collaboration in the creation of knowledge made easier. But waves of stories, narratives, rumours, panics, factoids, and opinions can travel just as rapidly around the capital assets of the world's communications systems, and in volumes many times greater.

## No Mistakes and No Learning

Democracy has grown up alongside capitalism since the industrial revolution. Modern democracy has a strongly rational element to it, yet it too leans on stories and narratives, transmissible by media, to find simple ways of explaining complicated events to electorates, and to provide competing views of the future. These stories and narratives must have a basis in fact, since in democracies anyone can check for obvious untruths. But programmes for the future, like manifestos and commitments at election time, have a large aspirational, promissory, element too.

In his political writing connected to his theory of the development of scientific knowledge, including *The Open Society and Its Enemies* (1945), the philosopher Karl Popper put forward a modest, problem-solving view of politics. That is, rather than pursue the utopian ideal of trying to create a paradise here on earth, or put off taking action until a promised revolution has dawned, small-scale practical improvements should be sought, which alleviate demonstrable suffering, or remedy identifiable social ills. In his popular introductory book *Karl Popper* (1973), former politician Bryan Magee drew the parallel between Popper's view of science as a problem-solving activity and this problem-solving approach to politics. Closed societies, where it is impossible to change political leaders without recourse to violence, tend not to learn from their mistakes; open societies can.

Magee's ideal, building on Popper, is therefore a situation where government policies, just like scientific theories, are put to a tough trial and error test: a public policy is "a hypothesis" to be tested against reality and corrected in the light of experience. It is better to detect mistakes and hidden dangers in policies by critical examination and democratic debate than to wait until they reveal themselves in practice. And the *implementation* of every policy needs to be tested too: and this is done, not by looking for evidence that policies are having the desired effects, but by looking for evidence *that they are not*. As in science, it is by finding errors that progress is made.

Now this problem-solving approach may well be the ideal for open societies to aim at. But if narrative politics goes the way of narrative economics it may not be encountered in practice, even in democracies. Why? Because learning from mistakes—the scientific method of trial and error—is no longer what is important. If mistakes have been made, political leaders may lose power rather than be commended for learning from them. Knowing this, *not* learning from mistakes, and not acknowledging mistakes, may be a better narrative tactic. Or, if mistakes have been made, they can be made the fault of others; or other political parties; or events in the world beyond, beyond anyone's control.

As observed by an earlier politician, Richard Crossman, writing his introduction in the 1960s to Walter Bagehot's nineteenth-century-classic

*The English Constitution*, the incompetent minister with a departmental muddle to cover up can still be kept in office for years. The louder the demand for his dismissal, the more loyally the "party oligarchy" will support him, "rightly calculating that more votes will be lost in a general election in admitting ministerial incompetence than in concealing it".

Democracies might, under narrative politics, change their political leaders and parties, following elections, and yet not learn anything. Programmes and projects can be begun and abandoned, because they do not fit into the new narratives of a new administration, keen to launch its own new experiments of policy. But if no lessons are learned, trial and error does not take place, improvements in policy are not made and errors repeat themselves. Party "oligarchies" can use narratives to shape the psychology of public opinion, with only tenuous links to the evidence of reality. Narratives, it goes without saying, need not be wholly true.

When it comes to the crucial role of finance and economics in capitalist society, there has, moreover, been much reticence in the decades since the end of Bretton Woods. Few elected leaders anywhere have had much to say at all about the operation of the immense modern global economy. As Henry Kissinger remarked in *World Order* (2014), the political and economic organisations of the modern world have become "at variance" with each other: the world's political "managers" have few incentives to risk their domestic support on anticipating economic or financial problems whose complexity means they remain the preserve of experts.

## The Unbearable Lightness of Being

So in the last quarter of the twentieth century, and into the twenty-first, the intertwined worlds of finance, the media, and politics have, to varying degrees, allowed themselves to become somewhat detached from the critical rationalism of the scientific method. Although globalisation, as it became known during this period, could not work at all without modern sophisticated networks of communications—capital assets based on rigorous science—the signals and content transmitted around these networks have served to promote more stories than science; and more conventional wisdom than knowledge.

The end of the gold standard under Bretton Woods did not, as some predicted, lead to an "information standard" replacing the gold standard, with vast numbers of transactions between the world's global banks generating knowledge, so bringing the supply and demand for the world's currencies into stable balance. The banks instead turned to speculating against each other's expectations of currency movements, and the standard became a permanently moving target.

Nor did global communications produce a global newspaper for the global village. Instead, competing media organisations and platforms proliferated, each with a partial view of the world, and stories and narratives designed to attract attention and advertising revenue to their own capital assets. Knowledge about what other people think is happening, and what they think might happen in future, and what they might do, has become particularly prized.

In the world of politics, the collapse of Communism, and the closed society in central and eastern Europe, did not usher in a new generation of Havels to build a truth-based politics for the open society. Drawing the deceptively simple lesson that the market must always be right, and perhaps believing that the world's largest financial institutions already know everything about the workings of the global economy, governments around the developed world sought to harness speculative trends to their own policies and economies, as tax revenues from finance accumulated and asset prices rose—signifying not economic instability and future disaster, but rather the blessings of the gods of finance.

After an enormous financial crisis, like that of 2008, when expectations of the future collapse, all the optimistic narratives justifying the boom in asset prices vanish into thin air, and the contrary emotions of fear and panic seize investment markets; then the economy; and then society. With a grasp on critical rationality enfeebled during the narrative years, handling a crisis becomes a conceptual grappling with the inconceivable. The main narrative metaphor in 2008 was that "a storm" had hit, as if out of a clear blue sky a severe and unexpected shock event had struck a peaceful world. But a storm is a feature of a weather system, and, as such, capable of scientific analysis and explanation. Whatever else a storm may be, it is not a collapse in expectations of yields of capital assets.

Democracies might be fortunate after a major crisis, as in the United States in the 1930s, and throw up a Roosevelt, with the energy and ability to counter a depression, reform the banking system root and branch and find a way to remedy the panicked fear preventing the return of economic activity. Or they may be unlucky, as in most of the developed world after 2008, when hardly any political leaders grasped what was happening, or, if they had a plan, were unable to remain in office long enough to implement it. Particularly unlucky seemed to be the United States and the UK, the main hosts of the crisis, on opposite sides of the Atlantic, where reforms were half-finished or inadequate, or not understood by enough of the population, and who within the decade slid back into populist anti-system political leaderships, frankly nationalistic, and protectionist in tone.

The next chapter will look in more precise detail into the nature of the expectations whose collective collapse leads to a sharp economic downturn, shattering the confidence in the political structures the economy supports.

## References

Augar P, *The Greed Merchants*, 2005, London, Allen Lane.

Crossman R, "Introduction", Bagehot W, *The English Constitution*, 1867, 1983, Glasgow, Fontana/Collins.

Hesse H, *The Glass Bead Game*, 1943, 2000, London, Vintage.

Kissinger H, *World Order*, 2014, London, Penguin.

Liedman S-E, *A World to Win: The Life and Works of Karl Marx*, 2018, London, Verso.

Magee B, *Popper*, 1985, London, Fontana.

Popper K, *The Open Society and Its Enemies*, 1971, Princeton, Princeton University Press.

Shiller R, *Narrative Economics*, 2019, Princeton, Princeton University Press.

CHAPTER 4

# What Do You Expect?

**Abstract** How long-term expectations in financial markets differ from short-term expectations in the normal, "real" economy for producing goods and services.

**Keywords** Short-term expectations · Long-term expectations · Money manager capitalism · Yields of capital assets

## The Role of Expectations

We saw in Chapter 1 that today's large global financial markets generally have some basis in a method more or less scientific, but that as they grow and develop collective opinion and sentiment about the future come to dominate. Expectations, in the form of the majority opinion of the market, fluctuate in the light of changing events and shifting moods.

What do we mean here by "expectations"? We all have expectations of some kind of what the future might hold. Sometimes they are based on personal experience; sometimes on what we have heard from other people. Sometimes they are backed by a solid scientific theory (that if we throw a ball up in the air the force of gravity will pull it back down again). Sometimes expectations are hunches; or subconscious (that the sun will rise tomorrow, or that we will wake again after falling asleep).

© The Author(s), under exclusive license to Springer Nature Switzerland AG 2021

D. Harrison, *Capitalism and the Dark Forces of Time and Ignorance*, https://doi.org/10.1007/978-3-030-78394-5_4

Expectations play an important role in the evolutionary theory of knowledge developed by Popper. Popper suggested that all living organisms have expectations of the world they live in, and knowledge is developed by the testing, or checking, of expectations by a trial and error process. Some expectations derive from previous experience; some (Popper thought probably most) are inborn, and are part of the adaptation of an organism to its environment. The very earliest life-forms—single cell micro-organisms—developed a capacity to sense light, allowing them to move into and away from sunlight, by a process of trial and error. This capacity evolved into the eye, and expectations of patterns of light and dark came to determine the lives of all successor organisms.

Human expectations are often based on having already observed certain events repeat themselves; although (as David Hume pointed out) just because something happened in the past does not, logically, mean it will happen again. We need constantly to check, or update, our expectations against reality. That is how knowledge grows. Scientific knowledge, with its rigorous testing and checking of theories, is a refinement of this same trial and error process. As Popper liked to say, all life is problem-solving: from the amoeba to Einstein is only one step.

We can consider expectations in the economy in two different ways: in the short term and in the long term. These correspond to Minsky's two different price systems, from Chapter 1; one for the current output of goods and services, and the need to recover costs; and another for valuing income flows from financial and capital assets.

Hayek's price telecommunications signals, transmitting useful knowledge round society, are features of the first system. Prices of the current output of goods and services—of what producers in the economy are producing at any given moment—depend upon those producers reaching an agreement with purchasers. The price reflects that agreement. In a competitive, decentralised, economy, few producers can control the price at which they sell. With the exception of a handful having a monopoly, or being dominant in a market, prices result from a negotiation between sellers and purchasers, with the outcome depending on who is competing to supply similar goods and services, and the demand expressed by who is purchasing.

Producers certainly have *expectations* that they will be able to achieve a particular sale price, based on their previous experience and general knowledge of the market, but they do not have certainty until an agreement on price is struck. In his *General Theory* Keynes called these kinds of expectations "short-term". Short-term expectations about what a producer can make from selling its output of goods or services can usually be adjusted in the light of sales results. Producers can in this way, relatively smoothly, adjust all the resources they use, including the amount of employment they make, as their expectations of the short-term future are confirmed (or not) by actual sales. There is therefore a testing of expectations, by trial and error. It is a continuous process.

This trial and error method is what distinguished the decentralised market economy from the central planning system of Communist Europe. Under central planning, output was not adjusted in light of the price purchasers were willing to pay, so it bore little or no relation to what people actually wanted. The result was that this kind of economy, adopted by the twentieth-century followers of Marx, ended up giving worse living conditions for workers in Europe than the capitalist.

The capitalist economy has thus evolved another way of solving the problems of production than the state trying to run everything. Marx believed that crises of capitalism were crises of over-production, with producers blindly driven by competition to diminishing profits, dumping surplus products on the market and laying off workers. Gigantic means of production and exchange, subject to powerful forces no-one could control, would periodically and catastrophically create and destroy themselves.

In the twentieth century, the adoption of competition policy and law in most of the developed world has curtailed this concentration and combination of producer power. From the earliest decades antitrust policy in the United States, and after the Second World War de-cartelisation policy in Europe, have broken up combinations and accumulations of private capitalist strength. Today, across the developed world, producers cannot lawfully fix their sales prices with other producers, and are not allowed to fix or agree commercial terms, or anything else that will affect the market, with other competing firms.

How short is the short term here? In a competitive market it is quite rare for prices agreed between producers and purchasers to stay the same for more than two or three years, without an adjustment or renegotiation. Long-term contracts exceeding five years' duration run into competition policy difficulties, and are difficult to enforce in law in Europe. So expectations of the future normally no more than a few years' hence are translated into orders for current output, permitting a producer to adjust the resources available to the demand it knows about. It is a balancing process, as the producer moves forward through time, along with the rest of the economy: the internal resources (and costs) of the producer are aligned to match the external environment the producer lives in, with messages about this environment signalled to it through prices.

Assuming there is a proper competition policy framework to counter what is, technically (and expressively), termed "market power", Minsky's first price system works relatively well in practice. Expectations in it can be tested and checked, through a repetitive trial and error process. Market power is checked—it does not become absolute power.

## Long-Term Expectations

Minsky's second price system is different. Prices here are valuing future income flows arising from existing financial and capital assets. They have nothing to do with the process of production, or the way current output is sold.

Keynes observed in the *General Theory* that when a firm wants to *add* to its capital assets through investment, for example to expand its capacity for production, by adding new plant or a new factory, it is subject to long-term expectations about the value to it of doing so. These long-term expectations look much further ahead into an uncertain future than the short-term expectations governing the sale of current output. And crucially, as a practical matter, it is *not* possible to correct them in the light of results. Long-term expectations, governing investment decisions by individual firms, are volatile and erratic in nature, and prone to shift around in short order.

It is this inability to test long-term expectations which is the key here. Unlike sales of current output, with the sale price providing an effective check, there is no simple or immediately effective way of checking expectations of returns from new investment, or the income flow resulting from it. Investment decisions are important for firms; are comparatively rare; and mean taking a view now about what might happen ten, twenty, or thirty years' hence.

What there *is*, on the other hand, is the stock market, and if a firm is of any size its existing, already-issued, shares will be quoted on the stock market, and bought and sold back and forth between investors. The stock price acts like a barometer, or proxy, for the current value of the firm. If it is high the firm can, in theory, more easily raise money for new investment (by selling off new shares); if it is low, it cannot.

But, as Keynes also went on to say, most investors in the stock market are not competing between themselves to estimate the actual long-term yields from such capital assets; but, rather, to estimate what the opinion of other investors in the stock market is likely to be in the near future. This is a process of competition nothing like the competition between producers to sell their output in the market economy. Some investors may well be engaged in trying to make reasonable estimates of the long-term yields of capital assets ("enterprise"). But most are engaged in trying to forecast the psychology of the market—which is "speculation". And the more stock markets grow and develop and become sophisticated, the more likely it will be that speculation will overtake enterprise. The stock market is therefore not a source of useful knowledge to check the long-term expectations governing investment decisions.

Unlike, then, with production, capitalism has evolved an *unstable* way of addressing the long-term future, ten, twenty, or thirty years' hence, which is the time frame applicable to new investment. Short-term price movements of existing stock, driven by crowd psychology, obscure the view of this long-term future. And when over-optimistic collective expectations collapse across the board in a major crash, so too does real new investment, and so too does the economy.

## The Open Society Under Pressure

There is a close conceptual link between the market economy and the idea of an open society. Popper wrote *The Open Society and Its Enemies* during the Second World War, deciding to write it the day he learned in 1938 that Nazi Germany had invaded his native Austria. Popper's theme in the book is the distinction between those societies, throughout history, where individuals submerge their identity in a larger group and those societies where individual freedom is prized. As he put it, "the magical or tribal or collectivist society" would be called the closed society, and the society "in which individuals are confronted with personal decisions" the open society.

The word "open" is important here, and used deliberately. For Popper, an open society is desirable. But the future is also open, as indeed is the universe itself. By this he meant that nothing is determined. His argument against Marx in *The Open Society and Its Enemies* was not so much economic—he conceded that Marx's criticisms of the conditions of nineteenth-century capitalism had much force—as that Marxism was determinist: it fell into the trap of "historicism"—a belief that inevitable forces of history move mankind along, and that it is more important to hasten the day of the revolution than to make real reforms and improvements in conditions as they exist.

In the post-war period since 1945, the market economy has been synonymous with democracy and the open society, in contrast to the planned, closed, societies of Communist Europe. The decentralised price system has brought together "divided knowledge" under conditions of change, beyond the reach of any single individual, and in this way deepened the division of labour in western market economies, and improved general economic wellbeing.

But alongside the market economy, democratic open societies also depend upon public institutions, to provide stability in the face of long-term uncertainty. One such is the system of law, constraining, for example, the market power of producers in the economy, through the system of checks and balances which is competition policy. Others are institutions for healthcare; for education; for social security; for police and public order; defence; public transport; and for monetary policy (that is, central banks). In most cases these institutions have evolved over long periods of time, perhaps even over centuries, through their own process of trial and error, as shortcomings in earlier ways of doing things have become clear.

Public institutions are usually funded from general taxation, and so, in theory, should be insulated from the boom-bust tendencies found in private investment markets. Not entirely, however: during a private sector boom, as asset prices rise, general taxation receipts are likely to be buoyant, and state expenditure on public investment projects easy to finance. Conversely, after a crash, taxation receipts are likely to reduce, and expenditure on social welfare and unemployment payments to increase. State expenditure on public institutions therefore comes under pressure too: after an enormous crisis—as after the crash of 2008—many states feared for their finances so greatly that they prioritised austerity programmes and saving even over maintaining economic activity. So states and public institutions became, despite themselves, caught in the tailwinds of private investment booms and busts, multiplying their expansionary and contractionary economic effects.

The temptation to revert back to a tribal or collective closed society appears strong when there is a serious breakdown in a major financial crisis, with devastating effects on the economy and political institutions. The personal decisions of individuals can appear all too meaningless if they are trapped in a declining or stagnant economy; or unable to see a better future; or loaded with debts secured on assets whose value has just collapsed. It can appear to many after a crisis (for which they were, after all, almost certainly not responsible) as if not just their governments but knowledge and rationality themselves have failed. Old magical ideas like reclaiming ancient "sovereignty" resurrect themselves. Demagogues arise and barriers are put back up. If personal decisions have no importance, collective identity might be a better bet: there is safety in numbers.

## A Chequered History

If we look more closely, what appear to be modern problems are long-standing in nature. Since the earliest days of industrial capitalism there has been trouble with financing its investment. The formation of joint-stock companies in the UK in the eighteenth century led to the creation of "bubble" companies, most spectacularly the South Sea Company bubble, which collapsed in 1720, and the passing of the Bubble Act that same year, severely restricting company incorporation, until its repeal in 1824. It was the experience of buying shares in the South Sea Company bubble which reportedly caused Isaac Newton to utter the remark that "I can calculate the motions of the heavenly bodies, but not the madness of people".

In the nineteenth century, legislation in the UK made the setting up of companies easier through incorporation; established the principle of a company having its own legal personality; and limited the liability of investors to the amount invested in a company—an important step. However, the need for finance on a large scale for major investments continued to raise difficulties: the financing of railways, in particular, involved mismanagement, fraud, and speculation, depicted in the form of fiction in Trollope's 1875 novel *The Way We Live Now* but found in fact too, in both the UK and the United States. Bagehot in *The English Constitution* (1867) noted that in the British parliament there were said to be two hundred "members for the railways".

Separating the management and ownership of business, by incorporating companies with shares owned by others, created new possibilities for drawing large-scale new finance into industry by selling off company shares; but also created potential instability by allowing those shares to be bought and sold in their own markets, resulting in feedback effects on the management of business. Stock markets, for the trading of shares in companies, developed from the eighteenth century in London, New York, Amsterdam, and Paris, permitting those who did not actually run a company to have a view about its prospects. This is a powerful mechanism: it is hard for companies to ignore their own share price, but it has little to do with improving the long-term expectations of yields from capital assets; or returns from adding to capital equipment; or real investment.

Keynes considered that the separation of management and ownership of business since the nineteenth century worked *against* the spread of knowledge about companies. Because ownership of the stock of equity in society becomes dispersed among people who do not manage and have no special knowledge of the business, there is a serious decline in the real knowledge of the value of investments by those who buy or own them. The stock market is subject to waves of optimistic and pessimistic sentiment, with no solid basis for a reasonable calculation, but rather a "conventional" valuation resulting from a "mass psychology of a large number of ignorant individuals".

Under the advanced form of "money manager capitalism" , prevailing in recent decades in the United States, the position has evolved a stage further. Minsky's phrase alludes to the ownership of most financial instruments by professional institutions like mutual and pension funds and insurance companies, rather than individuals. John Bogle (1929–2019), founder of what became the world's largest mutual fund, based on an index of the entire US stock market, has recorded the trend in *The Clash of the Cultures*: in the 1960s these institutional investors held less than 20% of the market value of US stocks, but by the twenty-first century it had risen to 70%. A minority of these funds adopt a long-term investment strategy, but the dominant behaviour continued to involve a high rate of trading activity, with a constant buying and selling of stocks, with the aim of profiting from the price difference between the two.

This process leads towards what Bogle termed the "happy conspiracy" of a "double-agency" society. That is to say, the agents who manage money (on behalf of the end savers who contribute to their funds) are in a happy conspiracy with the agents who manage the companies (on behalf of shareholders). Money managers want share price appreciation, to draw more money into their funds, and senior managers of US companies make sure to deliver that to them, since their own remuneration is linked to an upward share performance. This is the happy upwardly mobile world of "money manager capitalism". But it results in companies pursuing an essentially secondary objective (maximising the price of their existing stock of capital, ***already sold*** to investors on the market) of little relevance to their own future growth and development, or to maintaining their competitive position in the economy.

Hence we arrive at Porter's explanation in *The Competitive Advantage of Nations* that while in the immediate post-war period American capital markets provided cheap capital for businesses, from the 1970s corporate goals had shifted. Unlike institutional investors in other advanced nations, tending to view their shareholdings as nearly permanent and exercising ownership rights accordingly, American financial institutions came under pressure to demonstrate quarterly share price appreciation. This, plus an accent on corporate takeovers and mergers and short-term bonus payments for managers, undermined the competitive advantage of American companies. Rate-of-return targets to screen new investment opportunities were high; harvesting of market positions common. American companies fled tough competition with foreign rivals rather than fight them. "Money manager capitalism" thus played its part in sapping the ability of US firms to invest for the long term, innovate and upgrade to restore competitive advantage, for their good and for the good of the economy as a whole.

## Anchoring the Future

If the future is "open" (meaning that it is not determined, in Popper's sense) or "uncertain" (in the sense of the word used by Keynes: meaning it cannot be reduced to a calculation of probabilities) then the further ahead we look into that future the more open and uncertain it will tend to be. Current expectations about the distant and uncertain future are always likely to be precarious, and vulnerable to shifting about in line with current opinion, or current market trends.

Hayek was at pains to point out that the kind of knowledge prices bring together is practical knowledge, "of the particular circumstances of time and place", not scientific knowledge. But there are alternative ways of increasing knowledge. One such *is* the scientific method, which is common to both the social and natural sciences: this is the method of trial and error, of inventing hypotheses and theories which can be tested, and of submitting them to practical tests.

Could fluctuating long-term expectations be stabilised by any such method? Keynes's own writings give some clues. He suggested in the

*General Theory* that rather than relying on unstable market estimations, the state itself should take on greater responsibility for organising investment, because it is in a position to calculate the marginal efficiency of capital goods "on long views and on the basis of the general social advantage". In an article "How to Avoid a Slump" published a year later, in 1937, he went on to propose setting up a "board of public investment" in the UK, to make sure that detailed plans are prepared for large-scale public and quasi-public investment projects, to compensate for downturns in private investment. In this way, railway companies, port and river authorities, water, gas, and electricity utilities, building contractors, local authorities and the governing authorities of London and other densely populated cities should be asked to investigate what projects could be usefully undertaken if capital were available at particular rates of interest.

Keynes, therefore, advocated planning for investment, since if the state can control significant elements of public investment in the economy, it should be possible to offset the worst effects of erratic private sector fluctuations. He called for "acts of constructive imagination" by administrators, engineers, and architects, to create batches of large and useful projects, ready to be launched at a few months' notice in the event of a private investment slump.

Keynes's concept of the marginal efficiency of capital consists, as we have seen, of two variables: the current price of a new capital asset; and its prospective yield, over its whole lifetime. Expectations of prospective yield are not fixed but fluctuate, in line with investment market estimates. The state, however, needs to pay no attention to these fluctuating market estimates: it can maintain the same long-term view of prospective yields of public investment, year in and year out.

This, therefore, is a method of anchoring fluctuating expectations of the future. It does not tell us what expectations of prospective yield should be; but it would ensure they do not vary too wildly from one short period to the next. An analogy might be the role for the Bank of England proposed by Bagehot in the nineteenth century: that central banks need to stand ready to dampen unreasoning panics by commercial banks in the money market, by lending freely when other banks will not.

A further point to note here is that even though market estimates of prospective yields of capital assets fluctuate wildly, the evidence is that *actual* yields turn out after the event to be fairly stable. As Keynes remarked in speaking about finance, faced with the perplexities and uncertainties of the modern world, market values fluctuate much more widely than seems reasonable in the light of after-events.

In the many facts and figures assembled in Thomas Piketty's *Capital in the Twenty-First Century* (2014) can be found estimates of the average pure real return on capital in the UK and France from the eighteenth century to the present day. After deducting the costs of managing investments, Piketty arrives at this finding: the pure real return on capital has remained roughly stable at around 4–5% a year over this whole period, and in any event within bands of 3–6% a year. There has been no pronounced trend, either upward or downward. The nature of capital has certainly changed: in the eighteenth and nineteenth centuries it was most commonly land and public debt (bonds), which usually produced rates of 4 or 5% a year. In the twenty-first century there is a much wider spread of assets to choose from, ranging from low-yield property (and zero-yield savings accounts) to yields of industrial capital assets possibly exceeding 7–8% a year. But the average returns remain remarkably stable, over the centuries.

Other studies paint a similar picture. In the United States, Bogle has calculated that in the 150 years up to 2012 a combination of the dividend yields of US companies and real, after-inflation, earnings growth has come to about 7% annually (4.5% dividend yield plus 2.5% real earnings growth). This is almost exactly the same as the real return of 7% in stock prices—except that the latter, at any one time, can diverge from the underlying long-term trend because of the effect of speculation in causing price instability. In a 2017 study entitled "The Rate of Return on Everything, 1870–2015" a group of economists calculated that in 16 advanced countries, over 150 years, average real returns from both equities and residential real estate (measured in terms of yields plus capital gains) have been about 7% a year.

So although financial and economic storms have wreaked enormous havoc on capitalist societies in the past few centuries, it seems, in retrospect, that much of this ado has been about nothing. Collective expectations have become divorced from the real world, but the real world has not budged all that much. This then raises the pertinent question: what can be done to anchor the unsteady expectations of finance? Could Keynes's ideal of "enterprise"—where most investors make reasonable estimates of the yields of capital assets—yet acquire a second life?

## Back to the Drawing Board

Democratic governments of open societies have an interest in addressing such problems. Open societies permit peaceful change and reform. The really important question is, as Popper put it in *The Open Society and Its Enemies*, how to organise political institutions so that bad or incompetent rulers can be prevented from doing too much damage. And after a severe financial crisis, leading in the worst case to an economic depression, bad or incompetent rulers do often rise to the top, causing considerable further damage. If things go completely wrong, they entrench themselves and become impossible to dislodge.

After the 2008 financial crisis many incumbent political leaders in Europe were voted out by their electorates, although none had responsibility for the crisis. In the United States it coincided with a change of Presidency which would have happened anyway. The Atlantic region, at the heart of the crisis due to interconnections between the enormous US and European banking systems, became a zone of discordant policies after it, with the United States and most European countries pulling in different directions. Anti-system political parties and movements thrived after the comprehensive undermining of a whole generation of democratic political leaders.

So it seems we may need to revisit the question considered by Hayek in 1945, at the end of the Second World War, when the post-war Atlantic order was first conceived. Should the economy of the future be planned or unplanned? The evidence is that a decentralised economy, subject to rules to ensure it stays competitive, works well enough when it comes to the activity of producing goods and services—and better than the alternative. Even in the sphere of investment, not all investment decisions can, or should, be centrally planned. The problem is that, in aggregate, private investment decisions are *not* in practice decentralised, but become linked up to one another, through the powerful transmission mechanisms of the world's financial markets. The basis of valuation becomes one of common or social convention, rather than an individual assessment or reasonable estimate of yield. This is worse than central planning—it is central mistake-making.

## Motions of the Planets

Newton's remark that in a financial bubble he could calculate the motions of the heavenly bodies but not the madness of people was at the dawn of the capitalist era. The scientific method, where theories are put forward and tested by trial and error, has improved on mere expectations by creating precise instruments for explaining much of the universe in great detail. The industrial revolution itself was powered by this method. Where theories are proved wrong they are surpassed by better theories, which are in turn put to the test of experiment. Newton's own scientific explanation of the motions of heavenly bodies allowed calculations of their positions to be made far into the future, and seemed the final word on the subject for a very long time. But then in the twentieth century Einstein produced a new theory which predicted slightly different positions of stars in the sky, resulting from the bending of light in the gravitational field of the sun. Einstein's theory of relativity was upheld by observation in 1919, and remains the best so far: although Einstein himself was perfectly willing to see it improved on, if possible. As with the amoeba, the method of trial and error continues.

In the next chapter we will see why Newton was right, and why the madness of people cannot be calculated like the motions of the heavenly bodies.

## References

Bagehot W, *The English Constitution*, 1867, 1983, Glasgow, Fontana Collins.

Bogle J, *The Clash of the Cultures: Investment vs Speculation*, 2012, Hoboken, Wiley.

Jorda O, Knoll K, Kuvshinov D, Schularick M and Taylor A, "The Rate of Return on Everything, 1870–2015", 2017, Working Paper 2017-25, Federal Reserve Bank of San Francisco.

Keynes JM, "How to Avoid a Slump", 1937, Skidelsky R (Ed.), *The Essential Keynes*, 2015, London, Penguin.

Piketty T, *Capital in the Twenty-First Century*, 2014, Cambridge, Belknap.

CHAPTER 5

# Possibilities, Probabilities, and Propensities

**Abstract** Compares Keynes's pessimistic view that the future is radically uncertain with Karl Popper's similar but more optimistic view that the future is "open". The implications for politics and economics.

**Keywords** Radical uncertainty · Probabilities · Propensities · Propensity to consume · Inducement to invest

## "We Simply Do Not Know"

We have touched on the difficulty for capitalist economics of assessing future time. Production takes up time. Obtaining the yields of capital assets takes up even more time. Present day transactions give an incomplete and partial picture of the future, and yet they need to take that little-known future into account. In this chapter we will widen the lens, and view matters from a more philosophical perspective.

We encountered Keynes's ideas about long-term expectations in the previous chapter. In the *General Theory* the discussion of the financing of investment is in a chapter whose title is "The State of Long-Term Expectation". Where Keynes believed he departed from classical economic theory before him was in saying that attention must be paid to a radically uncertain future. The accumulation of wealth, and the use of wealth

© The Author(s), under exclusive license to Springer Nature Switzerland AG 2021

D. Harrison, *Capitalism and the Dark Forces of Time and Ignorance*, https://doi.org/10.1007/978-3-030-78394-5_5

(meaning whether it is hoarded without profit; lent out at interest; or invested in capital assets) involves considering a long-term future, but about which our knowledge is only fluctuating, vague and uncertain.

Classical economic theory, thought Keynes, might work well enough in a world where economic goods are consumed within a short interval of being produced: but not in a world where the use of accumulated wealth takes place in the distant—and sometimes indefinitely distant—future. (If we substitute the word "savings" for "wealth" today, to take account of the enormous growth of pooled collective wealth in recent decades, in the form of pension, insurance, and mutual savings funds and the like, we can bring Keynes's analysis up to date.)

By the word "uncertain" Keynes did not mean difficult to calculate, or improbable. He meant it in the sense that, in the 1930s, the prospect of a European war was uncertain; or the price of copper and the rate of interest in twenty years' time; or the obsolescence of a new invention; or the position of private wealth owners in the social system in 1970. His view was simple: "About these matters there is no scientific basis on which to form any calculable probability whatever. We simply do not know".

Working backwards from a state of utter ignorance about much of the future, Keynes built up his general theory of how the different economic functions perform. It is not possible, he reasoned, to force people to spend all their income on immediate consumption of goods and services. Whether unspent wealth is hoarded as liquid money depends on the degree of distrust of calculations and conventions concerning the future; the greater the distrust, the greater the preference to hold on to liquid money. Wealth not hoarded in the form of money might then be lent out at interest (but whether this will happen depends on the rate of interest); or it can be invested in capital assets (but whose prospective yields are also vulnerable to uncertainty). The entire economic edifice rests on a fluctuating and unstable base: the volume of investment depends upon two sets of judgements about the future (the propensity to hoard money and opinions of the future yield of capital assets), neither of which has a secure foundation.

The views of Popper, perhaps the twentieth century's most eminent philosopher of knowledge and science, might be brought in here. We have already encountered Popper's core principle: that scientific knowledge grows through the development of theories, and that such theories must be testable (or "falsifiable").

Although Popper had comparatively little to say about the discipline of economics, he too addressed the limitations of knowledge of a future which is "open", and not determined. He pointed out that, logically, we cannot predict, by any rational or scientific method, the future growth of scientific knowledge. And since the course of human history is strongly influenced by the growth of knowledge, it is impossible to predict the future course of human history. He thus rejected "historicism", such as that of the Marxists: an approach to the social sciences assuming that historical prediction is the aim, and that this aim can be attained by discovering "rhythms", "patterns", or "trends" underlying the evolution of history.

The inability to know now what we might know in future overlaps with much of what Keynes held to be radically uncertain: the obsolescence of a new invention; or the social system thirty or forty years' hence; or the prospect, or not, of a world war. And while Keynes referred to the lack of scientific basis for forming "any calculable probability whatever", Popper, in his various writings, described the limits to the scientific basis for calculating probabilities. In systems of mechanics, for example, there are often motions which are chaotic and which quickly become unpredictable: they cannot be reduced to probabilities at all. Statements about probability are also themselves hypotheses, the same as scientific theories. The central question is: are they testable? In other words, to arrive at a scientific basis of a calculable probability you have to have a theory which explains why the probabilities should be so.

So Keynes's position that regarding many future economic developments "we simply do not know" chimes with Popper's general philosophy of the limits of human knowledge. Keynes was suspicious too of attempts to boil economics down to models, saying that economics is a science of thinking in terms of models *joined to* the art of choosing models which are relevant to the contemporary world: it must be this, because, unlike the typical natural science, the material to which it is applied is, in too many respects, "not homogenous through time".

Keynes's explanation of how holders of wealth behave under conditions of uncertainty takes him into the realm of hypothesis which is the *General Theory*. This is indeed a theory, in Popper's sense: it provides a testable explanation of how different parts of the economy connect. And it is "general"—unlike the special circumstances of classical economic theory, where the future is not important.

We can look again at the two methods described by Keynes according to which investors operate. Under one method ("enterprise") estimates are made of the yields of capital assets throughout their whole life. Although Keynes does not say so, this is similar to a scientific method. A minority pursuit it may be, requiring a higher degree of intelligence, but it is by no means an impossible task. With all due regard to the difficulty of estimating the yield five or ten years' hence of (for example) railways; copper mines; textile factories; the goodwill of patent medicines; Atlantic liners; or buildings in the City of London (to cite the list of capital assets mentioned in the *General Theory*), there is at least an objective basis for supposing that yields are likely to be within a certain range, based upon the yields already obtained for the existing and growing sample of similar railways, copper mines, Atlantic liners, buildings in London, and so on. Crucially, it is possible to *test* these suppositions, simply by waiting to see whether the actual yields obtained over time correspond to the original estimate. By this kind of trial and error process, objective knowledge of yields of capital assets can be built up.

This time-consuming and arduous task is not, however, what Keynes thought most investors are remotely interested in; or equipped to carry out. Instead, the easier, cheaper and more immediately profitable method is to pursue "speculation"—forecasting the psychology of the market. As we have seen, this consists of trying to establish what the majority opinion of the market is in the short term, and taking positions accordingly: anticipating "what average opinion expects the average opinion to be", as it is put in the *General Theory*. Forecasting the psychology of the market distinguishes itself from "enterprise" by having no scientific method behind it at all. The shifting moods and sentiments of the market are not capable of objective testing by a trial and error method: like stories, narratives, or psychoanalytical explanations, they fall under the heading of what Popper classified as "pseudo-science": that is, ideas and notions which may well be extremely appealing and interesting but cannot be tested (or "falsified") by means of reproducible scientific experiment.

This, then, is why what Newton in the eighteenth century referred to as the madness of people, in a speculative bubble, cannot be calculated in the same way as the motions of the heavenly bodies: a scientific method does not (at least as yet) exist to test, on a reproducible basis, theories about how the psychology of the market might reach a frenzy of madness, and, if so, what the implications will be.

## An Efficient Pseudo-Science

Rather than accepting a position of ignorance of much of the future, or devising explanations of how people in the economy really behave in situations of uncertainty, much modern financial theory has, at least since the 1970s, conveniently assumed that the future is nonetheless calculable.

Underpinning this has been the dominant doctrine of the "efficient market hypothesis". According to this hypothesis, the primary role of a capital market is to allocate ownership of the capital stock of the economy, and the ideal is a market in which prices provide accurate signals for resource allocation. An efficient market is one in which prices always fully reflect available information, as it was put in the seminal 1970 article by economist Eugene Fama ("Efficient Capital Markets: A Review of Theory and Empirical Work"). This idea may sound faintly familiar to the reader. It is an echo of Hayek's telecommunications signalling system for prices, dating from 1945 and encountered in Chapter 1, but transferred to capital markets. The shift, although subtle, has had profound consequences.

Hayek's idea of the "marvel" of the price system related to producers operating in a decentralised economy, adjusting themselves to changes better than central planners in a command economy. But valuing the stock of capital in capital markets is different. There is, for a start, no production of anything new, since we are talking about a stock of assets which already exists. Nor is there any "change": buying and selling rights to existing assets adds nothing to the economy itself.

We should note, too, the shift represented in the idea that a market is efficient where prices always fully reflect available information. Information here is provided by the very act of buying and selling in the market, and the prices thus generated are presumed to provide signals for "resource allocation" (that is, decisions by the firms themselves whose securities are being priced, as well as decisions by investors as to which securities to own). There is a circularity in the idea that prices will be efficient when they fully reflect available information, since it is impossible ever to tell whether all information has been taken into account, or not. It is an untestable proposition, or (in Popper's terms) a pseudo-science.

Supported by this untestable proposition, enormous volumes of transactions have taken place in capital markets in the decades since the 1970s, signifying great restlessness in the ownership of the capital stock of the economy. Holding periods of ownership have become very short: from an average of around four years in the United States at the end of the Second World War to about two months by 2008. Estimating the yields of capital assets over their whole life has shrunk to the activity of a tiny minority.

A corollary of the hypothesis of market efficiency is that future price changes will be random. Since existing prices in capital markets already reflect all available information, only new information will change prices. Given large numbers of buyers and sellers in capital markets, new information will lead to random movements: and (statistically speaking) these random movements will take place within a "normal distribution", following a bell curve. This statistical distribution can be calculated, and therefore the probability of future price movements being with a certain range can also be calculated.

On this basis the riskiness of the activities in capital markets of the world's largest financial institutions, such as banks, were calculated in the early twenty-first century (using a method known as "value at risk"). Perhaps not surprisingly, this method was found severely wanting in the financial crisis of 2008: financial prices do not move randomly, but in the patterns of booms and busts, often interspersed with periods of calm, which make statistical extrapolation so precarious.

If we step back it is not very difficult to see why: rather than prices transmitting objective information about an independent process of change (as in Hayek) they are instead transmitting the subjective view of those in the capital market engaged in buying and selling rights or titles to assets which already exist. In the absence of a good scientific basis for testing the merits of collective opinion, prices can wander as far up or down as plausibility will allow—or further, if those in the market are sufficiently credulous.

## Two General Theories

Let us return to Popper's suggestion that statements about probability require an underlying testable hypothesis, the same as any scientific theory. How far is probability connected to finance and the economy? Keynes, after all, was concerned about the impact of radical uncertainty: of matters in the future about which no calculation of probability can be made at all: "We simply do not know".

However, years before writing the *General Theory*, Keynes also wrote a *Treatise on Probability* (1921). In this work he suggested that probability is related to knowledge: probability is the degree of belief it is rational to entertain about a particular proposition (for example, whether or not to take an umbrella out in an expectation of rain). The highest degree of rational belief, termed *certain* rational belief, corresponds to *knowledge*. "We may be said to know a thing when we have a certain rational belief in it, and *vice versa*". Keynes's *Treatise on Probability* therefore dealt with situations of imperfect or inconclusive knowledge, or knowledge where there is a degree of rational belief below the level of certainty. The *General Theory* then goes on to deal with future situations about which there is *no* certain knowledge whatsoever; and *no* means of calculating probabilities.

There seems little evidence that Keynes was aware of Popper's development of the theory of scientific knowledge, but Popper was aware of Keynes's work. In *The Logic of Scientific Discovery*, published in German in Vienna in 1934, but not in English until 1959, long after Keynes's death in 1946, Popper classified Keynes's treatment of probability in the *Treatise* as "subjective" (that is, depending on rational belief in a proposition), as opposed to those theories of probability which are "objective" (that is, which deal with the relative frequency of events in a series of occurrences).

For Popper, knowledge, including scientific knowledge itself, is *never* certain. It is always conjectural and provisional, representing the best theoretical explanation currently available. It is subject to trial and error, and if it is scientific knowledge it must be capable of being tested, or falsified, by independent experiment. Being personally certain or not of the truth of a proposition, as Keynes had put it in the *Treatise*, does not really matter: what matters is whether that proposition can be expressed in an objective form which can be tested by others. If it cannot survive testing it is wrong: if it survives testing it is (provisionally) right—although, as the history of science shows, it may only survive until it is supplanted by a better proposition in future.

A good half-century after *The Logic of Scientific Discovery*, Popper returned to the theme of probability in a lecture before the World Congress of Philosophy in 1988, published in *A World of Propensities*—one of his last works, even as the Communist system in Europe was reaching its demise, and the cold war coming to an end.

Classical "objective" probability theory, Popper reminded his audience, is concerned with the frequency of events in a series of occurrences. The probability of an event is the number of favourable possibilities divided by the number of all the equal possibilities. So in the case of a toss of a coin, the probability of tails turning up is 1 divided by 2, because there is one favourable possibility and two equal possibilities. In the case of a six-sided die, the probability of number 2 turning up is 1 divided by 6, because there is one favourable possibility and six equal possibilities.

Now, Popper pointed out that apart from games of chance where equal possibilities are specified in advance, in most situations in the real world possibilities are not equal. (And in a game of chance a die could be loaded, so the possibilities of it landing on each of its six sides are not equal.) What happens then? The unequal, or weighted, possibilities (or a weighted die) will still have *propensities* to give statistical results, if an event is repeated often enough (or a weighted die rolled sufficiently often). A general theory of probability should therefore include *weighted* possibilities: equal possibilities can be regarded as weighted possibilities whose weights happen to be equal; or, in other words, a special case within a wider general theory.

Popper then takes a step further. Weighted possibilities become propensities, with constant repetitions, if conditions remain stable. Propensities can be considered in the same way as fields of forces, causing mere possibilities to actualise themselves, and become real. Propensities are inherent in a physical situation, and, in a real changing world, situations, possibilities and thus propensities are changing all the time. They also may change if we—or other organisms—*prefer* one possibility to another, or if we *discover* a possibility not seen before. And our very understanding of the world changes the conditions of the world, as do our preferences, motivations, hopes, dreams, hypotheses, and theories. Even incorrect theories change the world; although, as he put it, our correct theories may, as a rule, have a more lasting influence.

Scientific laboratory experiments often need to exclude interfering or disturbing propensities, for example by creating artificial conditions, so that experimental results can be repeated at will. But in the real world it is not so easy: real apples are not Newtonian apples, subject only to the single force of gravity. When they fall they are subject to a range of forces and biochemical processes, and so we can only say there is a *propensity* that an apple will fall to the ground in a given period of time: it is impossible to calculate precisely when.

The "material" to which economics is applied is, therefore, as Keynes put it, shifting and not homogenous through time because possibilities themselves are changing all the time. And these possibilities are hardly ever equal. That is why precise or probabilistic calculation of the economic future is impossible.

As it happens, the two general theories complement each other: Keynes's *General Theory* of the economy sitting quite well alongside Popper's general theory of probability—his world of propensities. The *General Theory* is mostly about the demand side of the economy, which breaks down into two main functions: consumption and investment. Consumption is the use of income in the present: investment is a long-term process, where the distant future is more important. Keynes described these two functions in terms of the ***propensity*** to consume; and the ***inducement*** to invest.

The propensity to consume is affected by a range of factors, but Keynes's underlying idea is really very simple: people tend to spend most, ***but not all***, of their income on immediate consumption. There is a fundamental psychological "law" that consumption increases as income increases—but it will not increase by quite as much. In Popper's terms, it could be said there exist a vast number of individual possibilities in the economy. These produce a statistical propensity for the mass of the population, responsible for an important economic activity, to behave in a particular way. The result is that as the income of society as a whole increases, only a diminishing proportion is used for consumption—and the larger the income, the greater the margin between income and consumption. So the richer the community, the wider the gap between its actual and its potential production. As Keynes put it, "a wealthy community will have to discover much ampler opportunities for investment if the saving propensities of its wealthier members are to be compatible with the employment of its poorer members".

This, then, brings us to the crux of the *General Theory*. As society develops economically, and becomes wealthier, so must it look increasingly to invest to compensate for the diminishing part played by consumption. But investment involves considering the future and that future is always uncertain. Capitalism needs to have an increasing regard to the future if it is to survive, but it does not know what that future is. It is the weight of uncertainty hanging over the future which affects the inducement to invest—and in Keynes's view fatally, which is why the state has to take offsetting countermeasures when private investment breaks down completely, in a crisis. The necessary knowledge to induce sufficient private investment for the economy to function properly is absent.

This is then, fundamentally, a pessimistic diagnosis of capitalism. As the income of society grows, so society needs ever more investment, but so does it become ever more in thrall to the impact of an unknown future.

Against this, Popper's *World of Propensities*, in contrast to Keynes's "dark forces of time and ignorance" which overhang the future, is remarkably creative and optimistic. Propensities represent possibilities which have realised themselves, and possibilities are always increasing. Popper suggested that behind the growth of possibilities—in the physical as well as the biological sciences—there seems to be hidden something like a natural law: all non-zero possibilities, even those with tiny propensities attached, will come to realise themselves in time—provided they have the time to do so, and conditions remain stable, or repeat themselves sufficiently often over a long period of time.

Rather than the future being a shadowy place of uncertainty, as in the economic world of Keynes, in Popper's conception the open future exercises a force of *attraction* on the present, *pulling* mere possibilities into realising themselves, if conditions are kept right over a sufficient period of time. It is a creative process: it explains why new chemical compounds create new possibilities for further new compounds to synthesise: possibilities which previously did not exist. New elements, and new atomic nuclei, are produced under extreme conditions, a process which eventually allows life itself to form, which itself leads to an unfolding of even more possibilities. And as possibilities can, and partly will, realise themselves in time, the open future is, in some way, Popper suggests, present at every moment.

## The Cost of Living

In the world of economics the price system, as we have seen, can do a reasonable job of dealing with the short-term future. This is because expectations in the short term can be tested, through a trial and error process. But this system is not equipped to deal with a long-term more distant future: accumulated savings might not be invested in new capital assets at all; or they might be diverted into speculation over the prices of existing capital assets. There are too many shifting situations, and changing possibilities. The terrific stresses and strains caused by financial crises—too often the precursors of extremism and disorder during two centuries and more of industrial capitalism—also narrow horizons and cause societies to close in. They therefore serve to prevent new possibilities from emerging.

In an open society, where peaceful change is possible, public institutions can, however, evolve to address the impact of an uncertain future, through a process of trial and error. Public institutions can accumulate knowledge of events as they happen ("institutional memory"), greater than that of individuals. If the institutions are well-designed, they can adjust, or can be adjusted, to changing circumstances.

Public institutions generally have no choice but to cope with an uncertain (and open) future. In many cases that is their *raison d'être*—they exist to provide insurance, like public health and social security, against large-scale risks affecting society as a whole. Unlike private investment in capital markets, there can be no restless shifting about of estimates of prospective yield, or hoarding of liquid cash, or scope for indulging in speculation. If public investments in institutions need to be made, to fulfil a public purpose, they need to be made: the costs of *not* making them (such as a breakdown in law and order; or a breakdown in public health; or a crisis in the money markets) are far too great. The development by trial and error of public institutions carrying out self-evidently necessary tasks, within a framework of democracy, has proceeded in parallel with the development of industrial capitalism: it is the other side of the coin, so to speak. There seems to be no end to this process: new problems beget new solutions (or new attempts at solutions) and those solutions (or attempted solutions) beget new (unforeseen) problems in their turn.

To borrow Popper's terminology, we might perhaps say that the institutions of an open society can help keep conditions sufficiently stable to allow new possibilities to realise themselves, over time. Society deepens in complexity as new situations unfold: an open society can permit them to emerge peacefully, whereas a closed society does not.

In economic terms, as society develops, and moves ever further beyond the short-term consumption of all it produces, there is an ever greater need to improve the inducement to invest. The question, then, is whether and how public policy and institutions might help do this. This may be an extension of the traditional role of public institutions, but—as in other developments of public policy—it needs to be weighed against the cost of *not* doing so. These costs, become evident over two centuries and more of industrial capitalism, include periodic and devastating financial crises; a draining away of savings from investment into speculation; generally poor economic performance; and mounting inequality (because wealth accumulates and is concentrated if it is not invested).

Keynes himself suggested that the radical cure is actually to close off possibilities, by allowing an individual no choice between consuming his income and investing in the most promising capital asset presently available. When particularly assailed by doubts about an uncertain future, such an individual might, "in his perplexity", turn more to consumption and less to investment; but that would at least avoid the "disastrous, cumulative and far-reaching" repercussions of him spending his income neither on one thing nor on the other—neither consuming it nor investing it. If we enlarge the scale to the whole of society, the problem emerges clearly: society as a whole is not able to consume all its income; but nor does it devote sufficient of its resources to investment in new capital assets. There are too many possibilities allowing it to do neither one thing nor another: to hoard savings in liquid form against a rainy day; or to put those savings towards speculation over the price of existing capital assets—such as in capital markets, or in markets for property and real estate.

The consequences of all this, "disastrous, cumulative and far-reaching" as they may be, will be looked at in more detail in the next chapter.

## References

Fama E, "Efficient Capital Markets: A Review of Theory and Empirical Work", 1970, *Journal of Finance*, 25, 2.

Keynes JM, "The General Theory of Employment", 1937, Skidelsky R (Ed.), *The Essential Keynes*, 2015, London, Penguin.

Keynes JM, *A Treatise on Probability*, 1921, London, Macmillan.

Popper K, *The Logic of Scientific Discovery*, 1959, 1980, London, Routledge.

Popper K, *A World of Propensities*, 1990, 1995, Bristol, Thoemmes.

CHAPTER 6

# The Best and the Brightest

**Abstract** How the best and brightest contributed to the development of the private global financial system which grew up after the end of the Bretton Woods era, until collapsing in on itself in the first decade of the twenty-first century.

**Keywords** Hedge funds · Passive investment · Institutional savings · Prospective yield · Asset price bubble

## Hedging Your Bets

After the financial crash of 2008 the writer was invited by legal counsel at the European Central Bank in Frankfurt to contribute a chapter on competition (antitrust) law to a *Research Handbook on Hedge Funds, Private Equity and Alternative Investments*, published in 2012. The book, edited by Phoebus Athanassiou of the ECB, included authors looking into many different aspects of the "alternative investment" industry, in light of the crash which, as the editor said in the introduction, meant it was published at a time of unprecedented crisis.

In preparing my contribution I pursued normal practice, which is to attempt to understand the economic activity, and market, to which competition law is to be applied, to see how the two basic rules

© The Author(s), under exclusive license to Springer Nature Switzerland AG 2021

D. Harrison, *Capitalism and the Dark Forces of Time and Ignorance*,
https://doi.org/10.1007/978-3-030-78394-5_6

(prohibiting firms from entering into anti-competitive agreements and concerted practices; and from abusing a dominant position) might be relevant.

I thus became acquainted with the fascinating little world of hedge funds. Although it is true to say, as the *Research Handbook* makes clear, that hedge funds were not responsible for the financial crisis, they nonetheless represent an advanced form of financial capitalism which the crisis demonstrated to be highly unstable. In many ways hedge funds became market leaders, developing new ideas and strategies affecting the functioning of capital markets. In a financial services industry which, before the crash, attracted the best and brightest into it, and accounted for a high proportion of all corporate profits, they came to attract the best and brightest of all.

The point which struck me after I had written my chapter, absorbed all the contributions to the *Handbook*, and much related literature, was this: hedge funds are nearly always vehicles for accumulating, preserving, and growing collective savings, and very rarely (if at all) vehicles for turning collective savings into new investment, or the capital development of the economy. As hedge fund manager George Soros used to joke, for him an investment is a speculation that has gone wrong.

The point can be explained by considering the origin of hedge funds. Although there are today very many types and styles, it is generally reckoned that the first was created in New York in 1949 by an American named Alfred Winslow Jones, with only $100,000. The Jones fund had two features. First, it bought ("went long in") shares in promising US companies whose value was expected to rise, which it offset by also borrowing and selling ("shorting") shares in unpromising companies whose value was expected to fall, thus creating a "hedge" against unpredictable market swings. Second, having created this "hedge", or insulation, against market swings, it then borrowed more money ("leverage") to magnify the market positions it took. Now, while the Jones hedge fund confined itself to shares in US companies, similar principles were applied by later hedge funds to all kinds of financial products: bonds, futures, swaps, options, currencies, commodities, and so forth. The hedge fund run by Soros from the 1970s, the Quantum Fund, involved taking a global ("macro") view of inter-linking developments affecting the component parts of the entire post-Bretton Woods world economy: US stocks and bonds; foreign stocks and bonds; commodities (oil); and currencies like the German mark, the Japanese yen, and the pound sterling.

The hedge fund concept, therefore, is a way of counteracting swings in the prices of *existing* financial and capital assets, starting out with those traded in the stock market. Paying no serious attention to the hypothesis that there might be an efficient capital market, it presumes that the market is prey to volatility, booms, and busts—and pursues a strategy for dealing with them. It preserves and enhances savings held in the fund by ensuring they are spread in a portfolio which, by one means or another, corrects itself against, and if possible profits from, market fluctuations. If we think back to Keynes, funds are not being used for consumption (because they are saved); and nor are they being used for investing in new capital assets. In a minority of cases hedge funds may be vehicles for long-term investment in companies, but that is not their *raison d'être*: their *raison d'être* is to profit from changes in the prices of existing assets.

Now, on a global scale hedge funds may not have enormous macroeconomic significance. At the time of writing the *Research Handbook* in 2011, it was estimated there were some 7000 hedge funds worldwide (having risen from 530 in 1990) with assets under management of almost $2 trillion (having risen from $39 billion in 1990). This sounds like a lot, but $2 trillion is only a small fraction of all institutionally managed savings in the world, operating under what Minsky called "money manager capitalism", which includes mutual funds, pension funds, insurance funds, and sovereign wealth funds as well as hedge funds. Total assets under institutional management had already reached some $11 trillion by 1990, and risen to some $87 trillion by 2014—so over forty times larger than the hedge fund industry. They are forecast to continue growing strongly in future decades. Savings funds on this scale *are* of macroeconomic significance: a sum roughly the size of world annual GDP is thus being taken out of consumption, and most of it (on some estimates perhaps 90%) kept in short-term financial assets of one kind or another—and therefore not invested in new capital assets.

An analogy is a complaint Keynes made in the inter-war period about the large sinking funds for housing depreciation used by local authorities in the UK: these species of "corporate saving" were subtracting from consumption without adding anything to investment, being worth more than half the capital expenditure of local authorities in the early 1930s. Yet today's "corporate saving" far exceeds this in scale: $87 trillion of institutionally managed savings is over four times the size of US annual GDP ($21 trillion in 2020); over 23 times greater than all US gross private domestic investment expenditure ($3.7 trillion in 2020); and over 340 times greater than the average of $250 billion of new capital brought annually to US companies by issuing shares.

In this ever-expanding world of "money manager capitalism" the great intelligence of successful hedge fund operators, like Soros, is to be able to predict moves of the financial markets before most other operators. Hence the subtitle of his revelatory 1987 book *The Alchemy of Finance* is "*Reading the Mind of the Market*".

Soros has based his mind-reading strategy on his theory of "reflexivity". This holds that there is a two-way relationship between participants in markets and the economic fundamentals which those markets are valuing. In financial markets expectations themselves play a pivotal role: buy and sell decisions are based on expectations about future prices, and future prices are contingent on current buy and sell decisions. It is a two-way process, with feedback. Markets become out of equilibrium (or "far from equilibrium", as Soros puts it) where expectations of participants coalesce around a mistake, causing fundamental values themselves to change. Examples of this are unwarranted booms in stock prices, which continue until the mistake is widely appreciated by market participants, causing the price to crash back down to earth; and collective lending by banks against the same collateral (usually property or real estate) causing this collateral price to rise, until the mistake is appreciated, property prices suddenly adjust themselves downwards and existing loans become unsustainable, threatening borrowers and banks alike.

Soros's gift has been to apply this theory of reflexivity to real-life financial market developments, spot where a reflexive boom-bust cycle is building up, and take positions through his hedge fund in advance of where he thinks the market will go. There is a real-time record of applying this method in the years 1985–1986 in *The Alchemy of Finance*. He has not always been correct, and he says himself that he often sees patterns where there is none, but often he has been spectacularly successful.

If, again, we go back to Keynes, what Soros is doing is "forecasting the psychology of the market", to a highly sophisticated degree. Soros's *forte* has been to understand better than anyone else the processes affecting the expectations generated in financial markets, and the implications where those expectations become disconnected from reality.

Other hedge funds have different strategies, but the theme of taking niche or specialist positions in advance of major market developments is a common one. To do this, hedge funds often cultivate great secrecy, and charge high fees to those who keep their savings with them. While some are very successful, at certain periods of time, they are also unpredictable and can have years of making mistakes and losses.

New light on their unpredictability was shone by a wager made by Warren Buffett of US firm Berkshire Hathaway in 2007: that no investment professional could select a set of at least five hedge funds which could, over a ten year period, match the performance (after fees, costs, and expenses) of an unmanaged S&P 500 index fund (that is, an index of the whole US stock market), charging only token fees. The wager (of $0.5 million, the proceeds to go to charity) was taken up by a hedge fund advisory firm, picking five "funds-of-funds", which in turn owned interests in more than 200 hedge funds. Each fund-of-fund manager was free to rearrange its portfolios of hedge funds during the ten years, investing in promising funds while dropping those doing less well. Ten years later, at the end of 2017, Buffett easily won his bet: the final gain of the S&P index fund in the period 2008–2017 came to 125.8% (making an average annual gain of 8.5%); the highest performing of the five fund-of-funds was 87.7% (making an average annual gain of 6.5%); while the worst performing fund was 2.8% (with an average annual gain of only 0.3%). So an index of the entire US stock market, requiring no management and incurring very little cost, easily beat the collective, and expensive, wisdom of the best and the brightest.

If we think back to the original hedge fund idea, it was to offset unexpected swings in stock market prices by going short in stocks opposite to those expected to do well. But the same effect of neutralising market swings can be obtained simply by creating an index of the entire market: more reliably, and more cheaply. An index fund is the sum of its constituent parts: it removes the need to predict individual stocks. The problem of trying to predict which individual stocks will do well over a long period of time is like trying to predict which set of hedge funds will win: expensive and difficult.

## Passive Resistance

The unmanaged S&P 500 index fund which outperformed the hedge funds over a ten year period was set up by John Bogle in 1976, and the firm running it (Vanguard) has become one of the world's largest mutual funds. By 2012, index mutual funds held assets of some $2.4 trillion—more than all the hedge funds in the world put together.

Bogle (a friendly personal letter from whom in 2015 the writer has before him, commenting on an article entitled "The Logic of Price Discovery") can be contrasted with Alfred Winslow Jones, the post-war father of the hedge fund. Bogle started out as an optimist. He has recounted how, when in 1951 he wrote his university thesis on the new mutual fund industry developing in the post-war United States, he predicted, accurately, that it would grow; but disagreed with Keynes's view, set out two decades earlier in the *General Theory*, that among professional investors speculation ("forecasting the psychology of the market") would overtake enterprise ("forecasting the prospective yield of an asset over its entire life"). On the contrary, the young Bogle thought, portfolio managers in the new post-war US mutual fund industry would surely apply a demand for securities based on a steady, sophisticated and enlightened analysis: or, in other words, a demand based essentially on the intrinsic performance of a corporation rather than its public appraisal reflected in the price of its shares. "Alas", Bogle recounted in a lecture six decades later in 2010, the sophisticated and analytic focus on enterprise predicted from the industry's expert professional investors had "utterly failed to materialize". In fact, the emphasis on speculation by mutual funds had actually increased many fold. "Call the score, Keynes 1, Bogle 0".

By this Bogle meant that the vast growth in equity mutual funds in the United States—from holding $2.5 billion in 1951 to $5.9 trillion in 2012—and the shift from private ownership to ownership by large public conglomerates, have only served to strengthen the search for short-term profits through trading shares back and forth between them, in the hope of price appreciation—with the costs of doing so borne by end savers.

We saw in Chapter 4 Bogle's remark that the result has been the "happy conspiracy" of a "double-agency" society, where both money managers and the managers of physical US companies have become focused on the upward movements of stock prices: the former to attract new savings into their funds; the latter because it determines their remuneration.

So two distinct lines of evolution can be traced back to the fact that, in the post-war period, the accumulation of savings into professionally managed funds for investment has not (exceptions aside, like Berkshire Hathaway) stopped speculation from displacing enterprise as the driving force. On the one hand, the hedge fund concept has grown since 1949 as a means of taking niche or specialist positions in advance of market movements, with erratic success, and expensively. On the other hand, the index fund concept has, since 1976, permitted the entire market to be tracked, consistently and cheaply, so that as time goes by market movements smooth themselves out and become irrelevant. So we end up with hedging versus indexing; and active versus passive.

These defensive responses to the persistence of speculation as the driving force of finance may make perfect sense from the point of view of savers who wish to avoid the undesirable consequences: sophisticated savers who can afford the high management fees charged by hedge funds; or ordinary savers who pay the nominal fees of unmanaged index funds. But yet it should be noted that in neither case, nor in a world generally where money management is driven by speculation, are collective savings making their way into *new* investment by companies—or, in other words, the creation of new capital assets.

## Losers in the Gamble of Uncertainty

To go back to the point we saw Keynes making, in the previous chapter, the volume of investment in the economy depends upon two sets of judgements about an uncertain future, neither of which has a secure foundation. One is whether unspent wealth is hoarded in liquid money form or not; and the other is the opinion of the future yields of capital assets. The post-war pooling of accumulated wealth into large collective savings funds—in some cases mandatory, like contributions to pension funds—has added a further layer to these considerations, and certainly to some extent stopped the hoarding of pure cash, but not removed the underlying problem of the weight of uncertainty hanging over the translation of savings into new investment. So we need next to consider institutional savings —"money manager capitalism" itself—against the perspective of an uncertain future.

According to former investment manager Paul Woolley and colleagues at the London School of Economics, there is a split between principals and agents at the heart of this industry. Unconvinced of the efficient market hypothesis, or that financial asset prices continuously adjust to reflect all publicly available information, they start from the fact that in the real world people delegate virtually all their involvement in financial matters to professional intermediaries—banks, fund managers, and brokers—who therefore dominate the pricing process. But this act of delegation—from principals to their agents—creates significant mismatches of information. Principals—all the end savers and individuals who contribute in their millions to investment funds, like pension funds—have far less knowledge of what is going on in financial markets than their agents, the professional intermediaries. And nor can they be sure of the competence or diligence of their agents. This means that when an agent, like a professional fund manager, does less well than a market benchmark it is impossible to tell whether the underperformance is due to the manager's prudent avoidance of over-priced stocks, or is a sign of incompetence. If shortfalls grow, principals conclude the reason is incompetence and react by transferring funds to the outperforming managers—thereby amplifying the mispricing.

Woolley and colleagues at the "Centre for the Study of Capital Markets Dysfunctionality" (the clue is in the name) have used this principal/agent distinction to model the behaviour of modern financial intermediaries under the incentives of the modern financial system, in a steady stream of research papers and articles since the 2008 crisis. In "The Curse of the Benchmarks" (2016) the incentives of large fund managers not to depart too far from any market benchmark are scrutinised, and the reasons why they buy rising overvalued stocks from short-term momentum traders, with baleful upward effects on the prices of stocks. "Taming the Finance Monster" (2012) coined the expression "expanding disequilibrium" to describe the logic of ever more exotic new financial instruments, like derivatives, devised to deal with market malfunctions, themselves contributing yet further instability, and calling forth further exotic instruments, in a proliferating arms race.

Rather than financial prices always transmitting useful information, uncertainty of the future is inescapable. Just as it is virtually impossible for anyone to predict which group of hedge funds will do better than a simple index of the stock market, so it is virtually impossible for individual savers, whether in pension funds, insurance funds, mutual funds or banks, to predict which financial intermediary will do well, after costs. Individual savers can only rely on past performance, or set targets related to what the rest of the market is doing.

For their part, financial intermediaries are faced with an uncertain long-term future too. While it is always open for those who are independent-minded to form their own views of what that future might bring (by focusing on the long-term returns on the assets in which they invest), they have strong institutional incentives making it preferable, on the whole, to follow the "market"—or in other words, each other. Beguiled by the efficient market hypothesis that the very act of buying and selling financial assets creates useful information, intermediaries continue to trade with each other, rapidly and at great cost (so eating into the value of the funds they manage)—and with ever shorter time horizons. By the twenty-first century more than half of US stock market volume had come to consist of high-frequency trading, with holding periods no longer than a few seconds.

So money manager capitalism has led to a spectrum of frequencies, from the very short term—a matter of seconds or micro-seconds—to the very long term—a matter of decades—which is the time horizon relevant for the creation of new capital assets. The greater the weight of doubt about the future, it seems the greater the tendency to keep savings funds in short-term, very liquid, assets and the less to allocate them to new capital assets, or the creation of new fixed investment.

Even within new physical investment there are variations. As described by Alan Greenspan in his book on economic forecasting *The Map and the Territory*, cost-saving investments in the United States (i.e. simply upgrading existing capacity) require far lower rates of return than investments to create new capacity, where future demand is much less certain. Likewise, investment in physical assets with short life-spans (equipment and software) takes precedence over investment in long-lived assets, such as the construction of new houses and factories with durations exceeding twenty years. Following Greenspan's analysis, the greater the life expectancy of the investment, the higher the rate of return required to justify it. And, as we might remember from Chapter 2, firms in the United States have been found to have *higher* rate of return targets, used to screen new investment opportunities, than in other leading industrial nations.

In the *General Theory* Keynes likened the constant revaluing of old investments and commitments by the stock market to a farmer, having tapped his barometer after breakfast, deciding to remove his capital from the farming business between 10 and 11 in the morning and reconsider whether he should return to it later in the week. Under money manager capitalism it is as if the entire fixed capital stock of the economy becomes liquid and fungible, and the very idea of planting crops for future seasons the expensive hobby of a few brave eccentrics.

Hyman Minsky, the originator of the phrase, saw money manager capitalism heightening uncertainty at the level of individual US firms and plants. Fund managers, he wrote in 1996, had made business management especially sensitive to the current stock market valuation of the firm: they were an essential ingredient in accentuating the predatory nature of American capitalism. The lot of middle management had become more unsure; historic patterns of firm paternalism had unravelled; there was almost a chronic need to reduce overheads, and to seek out the least expensive variable cost. A combination of competitive pressures from cheaper transport and communications costs and an unwillingness to accept lower profit margins to sustain domestic products had decreased the assurance of continued employment by blue collar, white collar, and middle management personnel. Even though the aggregate performance of the economy was not bad, individual security had diminished.

So it is that uncertainty, not wealth, trickles down in money manager capitalism. Without sufficient confidence in the future to maintain an adequate flow of savings into productive new investment, it ultimately comes knocking on the door of the employees of firms whose own commercial prospects are shrinking.

And there are, as Minsky added, limits to how much uncertainty people can or will tolerate. If there are not institutional innovations to help offset its impact, "the losers" in the gamble which uncertainty imposes can become alienated, and "potential recruits for an alternative to democracy". Twenty years and a major financial crisis later, the US elected President Trump.

## Going Forwards, Looking Backwards

There is a whole world of practical difference between the idea that financial prices faithfully reflect all information—and therefore become *better* the more trading there is in financial instruments—and the idea that they only reflect ignorance and uncertainty of the future—and can therefore only disseminate that very same ignorance and uncertainty.

We could consider again the huge market for credit default swaps which, as in Chapter 1, gave no hint just the year before the crash of 2008 that the roof of the financial world was about to fall in. It is not technically possible for hedge funds to "short" bonds in the same way as company stocks, but an alternative technique is to buy credit default swaps as insurance against the value and creditworthiness of bonds issued by a large bank. The story told in *The Big Short*, the best-selling work of financial journalism by Michael Lewis, is how a tiny handful of hedge funds went "short"—or used credit default swaps—to bet against the entire US sub-prime mortgage market in the years before the crash, correctly calculating that the packaging of mortgages into securities disguised the poor quality of the underlying content, and the chances of default on them.

If financial prices faithfully reflect all information this kind of transaction should be impossible. After all, the information about the content of mortgage securities was known, not least to those banks and financial intermediaries who created them, and sold them on to investors. The credit default swap market was vast, reaching a peak gross market value of $5.1 trillion in 2008. It was almost entirely a market between financial institutions (dealers, banks and other securities firms), who themselves had access to the best possible information about market conditions.

What happened, however, was that a tiny minority foresaw a reasonable prospect that the rising US property market would peak and turn downwards, increasing defaults on mortgages which would in turn erode confidence in the securities which included those mortgages. This is exactly what came to pass, but it was *not* the majority view of the market before it happened. Financial prices, instead, reflected an almost unanimous belief that underlying property prices would continue their stately progress upward, supporting the sub-prime mortgage industry and all the securities based on it.

Rather than rely on the efficient market hypothesis, the evidence suggests we would be better off applying Keynes's concept of the marginal efficiency of capital to the kind of property bubble and crash which underlay the 2008 global financial crisis. For any given new capital asset, as Keynes put forward, there are two variables. One is its price (or cost of replacement). The other is its prospective yield over time, which is the return to its owner from selling its output, after deducting the expenses of doing so. The price is a current price, but the prospective yield is only a current *expectation*, susceptible to change, in line with the general state of long-term expectation of the future.

Modern financial crises—those since the ending of the Bretton Woods regime in the 1970s—are frequently linked to property price bubbles, fed by credit, whose collapse precipitates financial disaster because so much bank credit is backed by property. The Japanese bubble of the 1980s, when property prices increased five to six times in a few years before collapsing, is but one example. The Nordic debt crisis of the early 1990s, and the euro-zone debt crisis of the twenty-first century, are others. Property prices around the world had already been booming in the first decade of the twenty-first century, in advance of the US sub-prime mortgage disaster: doubling in five years in Iceland, for example.

Now, if we take commercial property (say an office block) as a capital asset, the price is the current price in the market of buying or leasing it. (Prices in property are in practice nearly always benchmarked against other property sales.) The yield is the rent obtainable for the duration of ownership, after deducting running costs and expenses. The extra ingredient in the US sub-prime disaster was the creation of mortgage-backed securities based on residential, not commercial, property. But residential property is also a capital asset, which can be rented out, and bought and sold for purposes of speculation rather than occupancy.

We can now quite neatly put Keynes's description in *General Theory* Chapter 22 ("Notes on the Trade Cycle") of the later stages of a boom and the onset of a crisis, based on the Wall Street crash of 1929, against a modern property price bubble. In the boom period itself (so in the first decade of the twenty-first century, in the United States and around the world) there had been "optimistic expectations as to the future yield of capital goods" (rents of property) which were "sufficiently strong to offset their growing abundance" (more property was being built), their "rising costs of production" (it was becoming more expensive) and "probably, a rise in the rate of interest" (making bank finance more expensive). So long as the boom continued much new investment (construction of new property) would show a satisfactory current yield (rent).

Disillusion comes "because doubts suddenly arise concerning the reliability of the prospective yield" (future rent), "perhaps because the current yield shows signs of falling off, as the stock of newly produced durable goods steadily increases" (more new property keeps coming on the market). "Once doubt begins it spreads rapidly". In "organised investment markets" (Wall Street, just as in 1929), "under the influence of purchasers largely ignorant of what they are buying" (mortgage-backed securities) "and of speculators who are more concerned with forecasting the next shift of market sentiment than with a reasonable estimate of the future yield of capital assets" (that is, most financial intermediaries), when "disillusion falls upon an over-optimistic and overbought market" (mortgage-backed securities) it "falls with sudden and even catastrophic force" (and leads to the collapse of Bear Stearns, the distress sale of Merrill Lynch, the bankruptcy of Lehman Brothers and a global financial crisis).

Aside from during a crisis, the concept of the marginal efficiency of capital is a more useful analytical tool generally, with greater explanatory power, than the simple efficient market hypothesis. In investment markets, like the stock market, rights to existing capital assets (stocks of companies) are traded back and forth. The prices of those capital assets were already set, when they were first created. In a stock market it is rights to prospective yields from those assets which are being valued, and revalued, and the dominance of speculation (forecasting the next shift of market sentiment) keeps values fluctuating, irrespective of the yields themselves, or the intrinsic performance of companies.

Can we then go on to apply the marginal efficiency of capital idea to modern money manager capitalism? Rather than institutional investors basing their business model on the actual yields of capital assets (the intrinsic performance of companies) the model instead is one of speculation (buying and selling with the hope of price appreciation). And institutional investors have, during the post-war period, become by far the main owners of stocks in the United States, by 2011 holding about 70% of the market by value. As Bogle has explained, these "newly empowered institutions" now hold 60–70% of the shares of virtually every US publicly held corporation, so having a firm grip on control over corporate America. This level of ownership creates great purchasing power, which is expressed in a demand for rising share prices, to boost the performance of the funds run by institutional investors. This demand, plus the incentives of company managers, on the supply side, to see their own share price appreciate (because it affects their own remuneration) gives a permanent upward bias to share prices. Even if share prices crash, as they did in 1987, there are likely to be coordinated public–private efforts to prop up a falling market—as indeed happened in 1987.

What are the implications? Bogle has calculated, as we saw in Chapter 4, that over 150 years up to the twenty-first century, US company yields have run at 7% annually, in real terms (4.5% dividend yield and 2.5% real earnings growth). It follows that stock prices which accelerate at a rate higher than this have an inflationary, speculative, and unstable quality. And a focus on maintaining such unrealistically high stock prices entails cutting costs at those companies—including the cost of any new long-term investment, leading to a spiral of decline in productivity, competitiveness, and good quality employment. The price of a policy of high prices of *existing* capital assets has thus become the cost of the creation of new ones, through investment. Savings, on a large scale under money manager capitalism, are being taken out of present-day consumption in the economy but are not contributing to future investment in new capital assets: they are being diverted, *en route*, to propping up old asset prices.

## Market Power and Market Bubbles

George Soros's theory of reflexivity applies in financial markets because expectations of the future play a powerful role. These markets are valuing rights to existing financial and capital assets, and the collective expectations of participants in the market affect those values, reflected in financial prices, in a feedback process. This kind of behaviour would not, as it happens, occur in real economy, producer, markets, subject to the rules of competition (antitrust) law. As I suggested in my contribution to the *Research Handbook*, if a group of producers, collectively, were able to affect future prices in this way they would enjoy "market power", and it is inevitable that legal steps would be taken to prevent them, on the grounds that competitive markets require each participant to be independent when setting its prices.

Price bubbles are a simple impossibility in competitive real economy markets. Something similar might be encountered, perhaps, in non-competitive markets, like those of the centrally planned economies of Communist Europe. With no functioning price system, and little or no matching of supply and demand, there could be booms in the production of some things (or, as Havel put it in his New Year's Day speech, entire branches of industry producing goods that are of no interest to anyone) as well as busts (shortfalls: so people could not obtain the things they need). But in competitive markets price bubbles would indicate something seriously wrong with the structure of competition.

Reflexivity is not, in fact, a feature of real economy markets for production. Why not? Because collective expectations do not play a significant role. The expectations which producers have about the prices of what they sell are short-term; are reached independently (as a result of competition policy); and are subject to testing or checking, by what purchasers are actually willing to pay. This illustrates the difference between Minsky's two price systems: one for the current output of goods and services; and another for the values of income flows from financial and capital assets.

Competition law does not make any formal distinction between these two price systems, but, perhaps because its origins lie in heavy industry and the concentration of producer power (antitrust law in the United

States; and in Europe the post-war coal and steel industries), it has some difficulty grappling with behaviour affecting financial prices—even if those prices have real-world consequences. This phenomenon is not collusion, as traditionally understood, but it does occur within a system which is relatively closed and interconnected.

Something similar might be said about banks, where Soros diagnoses reflexivity in the way banks over-extend credit in the same way against the same collateral (invariably property). Although banks are formally competitors of one another, they also operate collectively within a banking system. The core functions of banking (deposit-taking from individuals and the extension of credit to individuals and businesses) are cooperative as well as competitive in nature. Each bank needs to be connected to other banks to carry out these activities. The very creation of "bank money" itself in the economy (that is, most money) is a collective product of banks, not the product of any one individual bank. On a global scale, the very largest banks in the world (the "global systemically important banks", as they are known) are interconnected in many ways, including by means of the assets and liabilities they hold as claims on one another. The crash of 2008 was a collapse of confidence in this entire system, across the enormous Atlantic economic region, not just a failure of one or two individual banks.

Such a private global financial system is what has developed to replace the post-war public global Bretton Woods financial and monetary system, suspended in 1971 (whose intellectual godfather also happened to be Keynes). Rather, perhaps, as in the inter-war years, when some hoped that international cooperation between private companies would foster peaceful international relations, excessive faith was placed in the proposition that private financial interests would do a better job of managing the global economy than international cooperation. Soros, it has to be said, was not of that view. Already by the 1980s, although profiting via his hedge fund from currency instability, Soros was warning of dangers that returns from "hot money"—speculations on trends in international currencies, for example—could exceed returns from fixed, physical, investments; and fluctuating currencies could discourage physical investment because of the long time period to earn returns.

However, the instabilities of the post-Bretton Woods world were not addressed in the 1980s, or at any time afterwards, by competition policy or by any other form of public policy. The comforting myth of the efficient market hypothesis no doubt had its part to play. This private, *laissez-faire*, system was allowed to grow until it collapsed in on itself in the first decade of the twenty-first century, bringing down much of the western market economy and crippling its politics. The possibility of reinstating some kind of Bretton Woods regime, for the public good, is therefore considered in more detail in the next chapter.

## References

Athanassiou P (Ed.), *Research Handbook on Hedge Funds, Private Equity and Alternative Investments*, 2012, Cheltenham, Edward Elgar.

Bogle J, "America's Financial System—Powerful but Flawed", 2010, Lecture at Temple University, at johncbogle.com, speeches.

Greenspan A, *The Map and the Territory*, 2013, London, Allen Lane.

Lewis M, *The Big Short*, 2010, London, Penguin.

Soros G, *The Alchemy of Finance*, 1987, 1994, New York, Wiley.

Vayanos D and Woolley P, "The Curse of the Benchmarks", 2016, *Paul Woolley Centre Financial Markets Group Discussion Papers*, No. 747.

Woolley P and Vayanos D, "Taming the Finance Monster", 2012, *Central Banking Journal*, 23, 57–62.

CHAPTER 7

# Bretton Woods Revisited

**Abstract** Examines how it may be possible to return to a more stable, public, global monetary order.

**Keywords** Exchange rates · Debt · Equity index fund · Global monetary system

## Crisis Begets Crisis

As we saw in the previous chapter, in a world of fluctuating exchange rates returns from hot money can be greater than returns from fixed physical investment. In this chapter, we will go deeper into the nature of today's global financial and economic order. Launched in the 1970s at a time of optimistic belief in self-correcting financial markets, it is looking decidedly worse for the wear after the global crash of 2008. A disincentive to invest fits in with other phenomena indicating a distinct lack of self-correction in the order (or, perhaps more accurately, disorder) prevailing since the demise of Bretton Woods.

Before considering what might perhaps be done better, it is worth recalling what has not exactly gone according to plan.

First, the way in which Bretton Woods came to end itself precipitated waves of global instability. The Bretton Woods system, in place during

© The Author(s), under exclusive license to Springer Nature Switzerland AG 2021

D. Harrison, *Capitalism and the Dark Forces of Time and Ignorance*, https://doi.org/10.1007/978-3-030-78394-5_7

the immediate post-war decades after the end of the Second World War, rested upon a fixed link between the US dollar and the price of gold, and with other currencies' exchange rates fixed to the dollar (with permitted small margins of fluctuation of 1%). In 1971 US President Nixon broke the fixed link between gold and the dollar, under which through the post-war period the dollar had been held at $35 per ounce of gold. Nixon announced that, instead, the convertibility of the dollar into gold or other reserve assets was to be "suspended". "What a tragedy for mankind!", noted Arthur Burns, the Chairman of the US Federal Reserve, in his private diary.

He was not far wrong. An immediate but unintended consequence of the resulting fall in the value of the dollar against gold was a huge decrease, of 70% over the next two years, of the price of oil, *when expressed in gold*, received by the oil-producing countries who were members of OPEC. This reduction in the gold value of oil these same countries offset by a threefold increase in the *dollar price* in 1973, through the Arab oil embargo. Until then, the price of oil had been relatively stable for the world economy throughout the post-war period, rising only from $2.07 per barrel in 1947 to $3.07 per barrel in 1967. From that point on, the price of oil, *when expressed in dollars*, became unstable: going from $3.35 at the beginning of 1970 to $32.50 by the end of the 1970s (although remaining stable over this period *when expressed in gold*). Removing the anchor of gold to the dollar gave short-term domestic relief to the US economy by a devaluation, but introduced havoc into the dollar-denominated market for the international commodity of oil, the fuel of the world economy.

Ending the global monetary system set the scene for a sequence of large international financial crises, the first flowing from this same instability in the international oil price. Increasing the dollar price of oil had the effect of greatly increasing the volume of dollars earned by oil-producing countries, including dollars held in the accounts of large international commercial banks. These banks then recycled their dollar inflows ("petro-dollars") into new forms of lending, in particular to governments and state-backed entities in Mexico, Brazil, Argentina, and other developing countries. This became the first major international credit bubble of the post-Bretton Woods era, bursting in 1982 after US interest rates were put up to an enormous 20% (ironically enough, to combat the domestic inflation built up since the end of Bretton Woods) and Mexico declared it could no longer service its debts. The flow of inward commercial bank credit stopped, there was a reversal of flows, and a serious Latin American debt crisis ensued, lasting for about a decade into the 1980s.

Thereafter, each decade after Bretton Woods brought its own financial crisis, with booms and busts in asset prices. In the 1980s came the Japanese credit bubble, which burst in 1990 with the collapse of the Japanese stock market and property prices, creating a long and difficult recession. In the 1990s came the South East Asia credit bubble, pushing up asset prices and currencies in Malaysia, Thailand, Indonesia, and China, bursting in 1997, with sharp declines in currencies, stock prices, and real estate prices across the region. Ripple effects reached other so-called "emerging market" economies, causing the Russian financial system to collapse in 1998, and effectively putting an end to Russia's rapprochement with western Europe, after the collapse of Communism.

In the first decade of the twenty-first century grew the largest credit bubble of all, involving credit-fuelled increases in the prices of residential and commercial real estate across the developed world: in the USA, the UK, Spain, Ireland, Iceland, New Zealand, South Africa, and elsewhere. The precise mechanics of the sub-prime mortgage finance business were peculiar to the United States, but when US real estate prices began to decline in 2007 the collapse in mortgage-related securities and distress in the US financial sector, accompanied by the failure of Lehman Brothers, led to the near breakdown of the interconnected world financial system. In this book we have already seen how a decade of economic and political turmoil ensued in the Atlantic area, with effects still working their way through afterwards.

Perhaps insufficient attention has been paid to the geopolitical consequences of a world subject in this way to recurring financial crises. We saw in Chapter 2 that research over the period since the nineteenth century indicates that, as a matter of course, financial crises put great strains on democracies, with government majorities shrinking and votes for far-right parties increasing, making crisis resolution more difficult.

The analysis might be taken further. In the boom phase preceding a crisis, with asset prices generally rising, it is likely to be relatively easy for governments to fund public institutions and investments from tax revenue, in the name of public welfare. Expansion and international cooperation may well be the norm. By contrast, after a crash government revenues are likely to be hit, politics become polarised and inward-looking, and isolationist and protectionist forces gather strength. After the Wall Street crash Smoot-Hawley trade tariffs were introduced by the United States in 1930; after the 2008 financial crisis came "America First" policies and trade wars from the United States, and "Brexit" from the UK.

There is a lesson here for societies based on the mixed economic model characteristic of the immediate post-war period: they lack the proper vocabulary for explaining, or even the intellectual apparatus for addressing, the impact of international financial crises on their domestic economic choices. No matter how virtuous, enlightened, or wise those domestic public policies might seem to be, they can be undone by an international crash, beyond their control. A world of recurring financial crises is a world at risk of slipping away from international cooperation and back into cycles of mutually antagonistic far-right nationalism.

To add to the picture, the post-Bretton Woods regime has become a machine for generating large volumes of debt, both public and private. Under Bretton Woods, credit growth in any member country was constrained by the need to keep within the disciplines of fixed exchange rates: pressure on the exchange rate would come from too loose a monetary policy. Removing that discipline meant removing a cap on credit: fiscal deficits by countries and private credit creation by banks have ballooned ever since. Assets held by the largest banks had grown to be significant proportions of national GDP in the United States by the time of the 2008 crisis; and greatly exceeded national GDP in several European countries. In the UK they reached *five times* the size of its national GDP.

The result, however, has not been to increase investment levels, which would maintain productivity and growth: the bulk of bank credit has been directed towards property, or real estate, leading to the creation of asset price bubbles, as in Europe before the 2008 financial crisis. Central banks themselves responded to the 2008 crisis by enormous further monetary stimulus: with very low or even negative interest rates plus large-scale purchases of public debt, once again boosting financial asset prices rather than productive investment. There appears to be no way of switching off the cycling of this debt machine.

## The Original Idea

Although the gold convertibility of the dollar was suspended in 1971, it remains the case that, formally speaking, the Bretton Woods arrangements still exist. The Articles of Agreement of both the International Monetary Fund and the World Bank, adopted in 1944 at the original Bretton Woods conference and ratified by the governments of countries around the world, have not been abolished. Before considering what might be done better, we might recall some of the original objectives. Keynes was one of the instigators of the Bretton Woods system, and took an active part in the 1944 conference: although the actual result—a dollar-based system, with other currencies linked to the dollar—was not what he originally had in mind.

Below is a summary of Keynes's own thinking on the essential principles during the Second World War, before the Bretton Woods conference took place. It is taken from Roy Harrod's book *The Life of John Maynard Keynes* (1951).

Keynes thought that, first, the post-war period would need an "instrument of international currency" which would be generally acceptable between nations, so that blocked balances and bilateral clearings between countries would be unnecessary. Then would be needed "an orderly and agreed method" of determining the relative exchange values of national currency units, so that unilateral action and competitive depreciations would be prevented.

To do this there would have to be a "*quantum*" of international currency, not determined in an unpredictable and irrelevant manner (such as by the technical progress of the gold industry), nor subject to large variations depending on individual countries' gold reserve policies. It should, instead, be governed by the real requirements of world commerce, and be capable of deliberate expansion and contraction, so as to offset deflationary and inflationary tendencies in effective world demand.

Also needed would be a "system possessed of an internal stabilising mechanism", by which pressure would be exercised on any country whose balance of payments with the rest of the world was departing from equilibrium in either direction, so as to prevent movements creating an equal but opposite lack of balance for that country's neighbours.

There should also be an agreed plan for starting off every country after the war with a stock of reserves appropriate to its importance in world commerce, enabling it to set its house in order during the transitional period to full peacetime conditions. And there should be a "central institution, of a purely technical and non-political character", to aid and support other international institutions concerned with the planning and regulation of the world's economic life.

More generally, a "means of reassurance" should be supplied to a troubled world, so that any country conducting its affairs with prudence should be relieved of anxiety for causes, not of its own making, affecting its ability to meet its international liabilities. By doing this, self-protective measures of restriction and discrimination against disruptive outside forces would become unnecessary.

If the world is to cease its habit of generating a disastrous and unnecessary series of financial crises, capable of undermining even the most powerful and advanced of the modern developed economies, and throwing world trade, democracy and the open society itself into doubt, a way needs to be found to revisit such principles once more.

## Steps to Safety

It is no doubt futile to enter into too much detail into how this might be done in a book of this nature. Many suggestions have already been made; there are many possible ways of recreating a more stable global system. A practical consensus would need to be established.

But by way of illustration that this is not an intellectually impossible task, a sketch of one possible way forward is as follows. It would involve a cautious, step-by-step approach, building on technical developments in recent decades.

A first step would involve setting up, possibly under the oversight of the IMF (Keynes's "central institution, of a purely technical and non-political character"), a global, passive, mutually owned equity index fund, based on the world's stock markets. This step should not be too difficult to take: as we have seen, since 1976 there have existed passive equity index funds in the United States, in their simplest form based on the S&P 500 stock index. The technical issue is merely how then to create a truly global fund, encompassing the main quoted companies (say the 500 largest) around the world. This passive index fund could be taken as a good proxy of the world's main productive assets—the best in practice there is likely to be. We saw in the previous chapter how, by representing the entire market, a passive index fund has produced superior, and more predictable, returns over time than even the best and brightest of the asset management industry.

The ownership structure could also, as in the case of the original (and so far unique) equity index fund, created by Bogle in the United States, be truly mutual. This means that the fund, including its management, is owned entirely by its own members, not by a separate profit-seeking company. As well as establishing control, this entails costs being kept to the minimum: the fund does no more, or less, than track the progress of the companies comprising the index on which it is based. The evidence in the United States is, as we saw in the previous chapter, that in the period 2008–2017 an S&P index fund made an average annual gain of 8.5%. In the whole period from its inception in 1976 to 2011 Bogle recorded the annual return of the Vanguard 500 Index Fund as 10.4%—almost exactly the same as the S&P 500 index itself (10.6%).

It is certainly possible that, because of loose monetary policy, returns in recent decades have been skewed somewhat on the high side in the United States. As we have also seen, Bogle has worked out that in the previous 150 years up to 2012 US companies have historically averaged returns of about 7% annually. And average pure real returns on capital—in whatever form—appear to have been about 4–5% a year since the eighteenth century, in both the UK and France. Taking all factors into account, a global equity index fund, based on productive assets, could perhaps expect average annual real returns in the region of 7%, plus or minus a percentage point or so.

The mutual, cooperative, nature of the ownership of such an equity index fund might then be put to new and creative use. One way would be to encourage private debt reduction, by voluntary agreement. Holders, like commercial banks, of stocks of excessive unserviceable or non-performing private debt could, along the lines of previous international debt restructuring schemes, be induced to swap their holdings of low-interest debt for minority shares, and membership, of the (more remunerative) global equity index fund, in proportions yet to be negotiated.

Similarly, central banks could exchange debt assets like the government bonds bought, in vast numbers, under quantitative easing schemes since the 2008 financial crisis for *majority* shares, or membership, of the global equity index fund, in proportions again to be agreed.

Once a sufficient number of central banks have become majority owner-members of the global equity index fund we may then have, as

Keynes put it, the makings of a "*quantum*" of international currency, neither determined in an unpredictable and irrelevant manner, such as by the technical progress of the gold industry, nor subject to large variations depending on individual countries' gold reserve policies. The *quantum* would be their shares in an index representing the productive assets of the world. This is similar to an idea put forward by Robert Pringle (chairman and founder of *Central Banking* journal) in his book *The Money Trap* in 2012, drawing on work by the German monetary economist Wolfram Engels (in *The Optimal Monetary Unit*, 1981). A class of shares in the global equity index fund would be interchangeable between central banks (only): creating a form of intra-central bank money based not on gold, but on real productive assets.

With this central bank money as the common denominator, a group of central banks could, if they wished, use existing central bank currency swap arrangements progressively to narrow permitted fluctuation margins of the exchange rates of their respective currencies—perhaps, but not necessarily, at the same time as global interest rates are gradually raised back to normal levels. In practice, this process could start between a few closely connected economies (such as those of the United States and Europe, and perhaps Japan) and be widened over time to other currencies. Cooperation between the US Federal Reserve and the European Central Bank, covering the enormous Atlantic area and economy, responsible for a significant fraction of global GDP, would be a good beginning.

As a more stable monetary framework is gradually bolted into place, attention could then turn to the management of the international economy in ways suggested by Keynes in 1943, but conspicuously missing since the suspension of dollar/gold convertibility in the 1970s. One is to be able to modulate policy to offset deflationary and inflationary tendencies in effective world demand. If we take effective demand to consist of Keynes's two main variables (which are consumption and investment) it is evident that debt-driven consumption has seized hold of the Atlantic region since the end of the Bretton Woods system in the 1970s, to the detriment of investment in new capital assets. Since the financial crisis of 2008 the tendency has been mildly deflationary (whereas in the 1970s it was inflationary).

Reducing the stock of public and private debt may have some effects on consumption, to which careful attention would need to be paid. However, the main variable in effective world demand is that of investment in new capital assets, which the current post-Bretton Woods arrangements do nothing to encourage and everything to discourage. Credit and savings have, on the contrary, been diverted instead to speculation over the prices of *existing* assets, leading to repeated asset price booms and busts.

So one question is how then to reconnect the world's ever-growing stock of institutionally managed savings (at $87 trillion as big as world annual GDP, and forecast to grow yet bigger) with new productive investment. One way to anchor these savings would be to offer funds access to the (relatively stable and remunerative) global equity index fund, as a safety net, ***provided that*** they first committed at least a proportion of their resources to new productive investment, so helping a return to investment-driven growth.

An obvious candidate for new investment on both sides of the Atlantic, and indeed around the world, is in large-scale re-equipment and decarbonisation of the economy in the face of climate change. Encouraging a proportion of today's large savings funds to shift away from speculation and towards real investment could be helped by co-investing in suitable projects with public bodies, either national or international in nature (like the European Investment Bank, or the World Bank). A combined large-scale public/private investment initiative of this kind could do much to boost effective demand, and shift the balance away from debt-driven consumption. If tendencies become inflationary as a result of increased investment, there is ample scope for today's extremely lax monetary policy to be tightened.

In this way an anchor would be created for the private global financial system developed since the 1970s, which has proved to be far from self-correcting. It would incorporate a correcting or balancing mechanism designed to meet what Keynes called the actual current requirements of world commerce.

Over the long term, and with experience, holdings of intra-central bank money between central banks might themselves be varied to offset deflationary or inflationary trends. And equally, over the long term, if there is sufficient agreement between central banks and populations, money in circulation itself, as well as central bank money, could come to be backed by real assets.

## A Few Pieces of Paper

All the above is by way of illustration only. Other routes to stability are conceivable. What may perhaps seem surprising is that such steps do not necessarily require any fresh treaty to be negotiated and ratified, and are compatible with the Bretton Woods agreements as they already stand.

In 1971 the gold convertibility of the dollar was suspended, and the 1944 Articles of Agreement of the IMF were later modified to preclude using gold as a denominator of currency; but the formal objective remains to this very day to have a stable system of exchange rates—just as in 1944. According to IMF Article IV, Section 1, "each member undertakes to collaborate with the Fund and other members to assure orderly exchange arrangements and to promote a stable system of exchange rates". Even though IMF rules require an 85% majority vote to move to a global system, more limited arrangements, agreed between groups of countries, are expressly permitted.

As we have seen, Keynes himself was not keen on gold as a denominator, it being subject to the ups and downs of the gold industry, or gold reserve policies of individual countries. And it was the divergence between the growing surplus of international dollars held outside the United States against the finite stock of gold held in the United States which led Nixon to suspend the convertibility of the dollar into gold in 1971. A denominator based on the world's real productive assets would side-step this problem.

Returning to a system whose defects have been corrected may in practice entail little more in terms of legal formalities than a letter of confirmation, or statement of intent, between the parties who wish to participate.

Is an initiative of this nature—or indeed a reform of any nature—worth undertaking? If the hallmark of an open society is an ability to learn from its mistakes, the deep lesson is surely that the experiment of suspending the Bretton Woods arrangements has been a failure. Decades of low growth, high debt and economic and financial crises since the 1970s have undermined the foundations of the post-war settlement, and the economic policies which pulled the world out of the ruins of the Great Depression and the Second World War. No country has been immune and no country has benefited. Instability has bred instability. Time horizons have shortened. Long-term investment has not taken place, while measures of self-protection from disruptive outside forces have proliferated.

As at the end of the Second World War, a troubled world could once more do with a stiff dose of collective stability, guidance, and leadership.

## References

Engels W, *The Optimal Monetary Unit*, 1981, Frankfurt, Campus Verlag.
Harrod R, *The Life of John Maynard Keynes*, 1951, London, Macmillan.
Pringle R, *The Money Trap*, 2012, 2014, Basingstoke, Palgrave Macmillan.

CHAPTER 8

# Selling England by the Pound

**Abstract** Examines the UK's own troubled post-war relationship with both the global monetary order and its own European neighbours.

**Keywords** Brexit · Underinvestment · Inequality · Monetary union · Sovereignty

## Decline and Fall

During the Second World War Keynes was a member of the UK Treasury, and Keynes's plan for the Bretton Woods summit was issued as an official White Paper in the name of the UK Government. Yet after the war the UK did not live up to the hopes of those planning the post-war world. Having helped lay the foundations of international economic cooperation, the UK came to retreat over time from upholding and defending it, reaching perhaps the nadir in the twenty-first century of giving notice in 2017 to leave the legal structures of the European Union. As put by former US Ambassador Anthony Gardner in *Stars with Stripes* (2020): "Brexit is perhaps one of the greatest acts of self-harm committed by any country in living memory". How could such a spectacular falling away from international economic influence have taken place? This chapter will attempt a brief explanation, drawing on the themes of this book.

© The Author(s), under exclusive license to Springer Nature Switzerland AG 2021

D. Harrison, *Capitalism and the Dark Forces of Time and Ignorance*, https://doi.org/10.1007/978-3-030-78394-5_8

It is worth, first, putting Keynes's ideas for a cooperative monetary and economic system into context. The story goes back to Lend-Lease, the 1941 agreement in the Second World War under which the United States supplied war material to the UK, in its role as the "great arsenal of democracy" (Roosevelt's expression). As consideration for Lend-Lease, the United States required that the UK pledge not to discriminate against American goods after the war. This meant that planning for a post-war monetary order meant allowing payments for international trade to resume too, while avoiding trade discrimination and imbalances. For the United States, the removal of "imperial preference" was an objective in itself: this was the system in place since the 1930s, under which Britain and its pre-war empire gave preferential trade tariffs to one another. Monetary cooperation was therefore part of a wider picture, aimed at reforming the world economic system.

The Bretton Woods monetary conference duly took place in 1944, and the monetary and financial agreements, including the setting up of the International Monetary Fund and the World Bank, were ratified a year later. But the parallel plan for creating an International Trade Organisation to govern global trade failed to be ratified by the United States and, instead, the provisional 1947 General Agreement on Tariffs and Trade applied during the post-war decades. The UK's system of "imperial preference" did not disappear, but lived on in attenuated form during this period.

Although Brexit in the twenty-first century was certainly not inevitable, a series of policy errors and missteps in the years before it prepared the ground. Financial crises, when they come, invariably attack fault-lines within societies, putting enormous stress on existing weak points. The collapse in confidence in economic and political establishments, common across the Atlantic region in the decade after the global financial crisis of 2008, affected the United States and the UK particularly badly, the twin hosts of major financial centres. The election of Trump, and the UK's isolation from the rest of democratic Europe in its referendum, both in 2016, flowed from the crisis of 2008 and its aftermath, amplifying economic and social difficulties of a long-standing nature.

## Going Round in Circles

By the end of the Second World War, in 1945, Britain was in dire economic straits, with enormous debts. The end of the war brought the unwelcome immediate end of Lend-Lease, sooner than expected. Keynes's last task, before his death in 1946, was to negotiate a large loan from the United States, to tide the UK over the transition to a peacetime economy.

But post-war reconstruction in Britain, after the death of Keynes, lacked purpose and strategy. In 1947 the US inaugurated the Marshall Plan, to stave off complete economic collapse in western Europe. The UK, like other countries, was eligible for Marshall Plan aid, and indeed received a large share: $2.7 billion out of total aid of $12.3 billion from 1948 to 1951. What the UK did not do was use Marshall aid for investment on the badly needed modernisation of its economy. Instead, aid was used to pay for imports, to maintain the dollar reserves of the international sterling area (whose members were empire and Commonwealth countries) and to reduce public debt.

By contrast, the US emerged from the Second World War with a large powerful war economy, which it then retooled for the civilian production which would propel its post-war boom decades. France, for its part, used Marshall Plan aid to support a domestic modernisation plan, involving directed investment into key sectors. West Germany became eligible for Marshall Plan aid from 1948, and used funds for imported goods and investment in capital industries. Germany's current long-term large development bank, the KfW, was originally set up to invest Marshall Plan funds.

The lack of investment, and failure to modernise by comparison with the United States, or other similar-sized European countries, became hallmarks of the British economy. By the 1950s the UK was being overtaken by other western European economies, and in the 1960s its growth rates were well below the European average.

Having started out badly after the war, the pattern of chronic underinvestment persisted. In the twenty-first century, studies by the London School of Economics Growth Commission (in 2013) and then the UK 2070 Commission (in 2019) reported, respectively, that investment failure is "the UK's fundamental problem" and that "the UK's problem is that it is simply investing far too little especially when compared with other similar nations". As the UK 2070 Commission found, total investment as a percentage of GDP, expressed as gross fixed capital formation, had been for decades both declining and running at a lower level in the UK than in France, the United States, Germany, or the G7 average. Low levels of total investment, and skewed patterns of what investment there was, contributed to high levels of regional inequality, making the UK one of the most regionally unbalanced countries in the industrialised world. By the twenty-first century disparities within the UK had become greater, on most measures, than in Germany after unification following the end of Communism.

What went wrong? It was as if the basic message of the *General Theory* went unread in the UK. Apart from the missed opportunity of Marshall aid, there was no post-war public investment or modernisation plan or a public or development institution of any kind which might carry out long-term investment projects in the UK. Nothing like Keynes's idea, mentioned in Chapter 4, of a "board of public investment", ever saw the light of day, to offset private sector investment shortfalls by bringing forward large-scale plans for public investment. Nor, unlike almost every other European economy, did the UK set up a development bank to carry out large-scale investment projects; or use (say) the North Sea oil revenues coming on stream from the 1970s in a sovereign wealth fund, like Norway.

The main UK public intervention in the economy took place in the immediate post-war period, but consisted of transferring large parts of the economy (over a tenth of UK GDP) from private to state ownership. In the period 1947–1949 the coal and steel, railway, electricity and gas industries were all nationalised. No investment plan or strategy accompanied nationalisation, however; and the poor performance of the nationalised industries caused the entire policy simply to be reversed four decades later, in the 1980s and 1990s, when "privatisation" replaced "nationalisation". The Marxist argument over who controls production—the "commanding heights" of the British economy, as they were termed in the post-war period—diverted attention away from the point Keynes had made that it is not production, but *investment*, which the state needs to keep under control.

By the twenty-first century the cumulative effects of decades of neglect had taken their toll. The analysis of the UK 2070 Commission in 2019 provides an instructive insight into the way events unfolded over the preceding fifty years. Public investment *did* take place over this period, but was concentrated in London and the wider south east of England. This concentration applied across the board, to every field of expenditure: whether to research and development, culture, sport, the arts, national administration, national media, or military expenditure. By an "unstated but countervailing" regional policy, public investment in this way reinforced past areas of growth, and fast-growing places moved to the front of the queue for more public investment. Private investment, for its part, tended to follow public investment. Continued increases in property values, often arising from public investment in the necessary infrastructure, fed social and economic inequality in wealth and opportunity. Bank credit for private investment, dominated by credit for property, flowed to already prosperous regions like London and the south east, and in so doing widened disparities by raising prices in prosperous areas, creating barriers to social mobility within the UK.

Ironically, in light of Brexit, only EU regional funds and the European Investment Bank exhibited much in the way of a coherent policy and longevity: from 1973 the EIB invested £108 billion in the UK, and funding from EU programmes was critical to the successful regeneration of the cities of Glasgow and Liverpool.

So the UK veered between one policy extreme and another in the post-war period and for the remainder of the twentieth century: from the state taking ownership of large segments of the productive economy to it relinquishing ownership while abdicating any attempt to manage investment, following instead the unwritten rules of an unstated policy. Under the *laissez-faire* approach of so-called neo-liberalism, the market was left to run production and let investment take its chances. A two-tier economy resulted, part of it internationally competitive and receiving the lion's share of what investment there was, part of it not: and a growing divergence between the two, reflected in asset prices, and in particular property prices. The UK became a case study aptly illustrating Keynes's observation, in Chapter 1, that "the duty of ordering the current volume of investment cannot safely be left in private hands".

## Catching Up

The absence of post-war modernisation and reconstruction had its effect on the UK's integration into the rest of the mainstream western European economy, which rebounded strongly after the injection of Marshall Plan funds from 1948 onwards. The UK did not participate in the early efforts to unify the conditions of economic production and exchange in western Europe, through the European Coal and Steel Community from 1951, and then the Common Market from 1957. Having nationalised coal and steel in the late 1940s, the idea of transferring oversight of these industries from a national to an international level lay outside the realm of the politically conceivable. The UK decision not to join the Common Market a few years later is less easy to explain. Decisive economic considerations recorded at the time were the need to *protect* British industry from European competition; the fear of weakening economic links with the Commonwealth and colonies; and the fear that a European common market would be incompatible with worldwide free trade and payments. The UK system of imperial preference, dating from before the war, remained in place: even into the 1960s the bulk of British exports continued to go to the protected markets of the old empire and Commonwealth.

The internal failure to modernise through investment, combined with the external failure to adapt to European competitive markets, led to the UK being overtaken economically. In the rest of post-Marshall Plan Europe there was an investment-led economic boom through the 1950s and 1960s, persisting until economic dislocation came with the ending of the Bretton Woods system in the 1970s. But there was no German-style post-war "economic miracle" in the UK. Nor were there French-style "thirty glorious years". There was only economic growth running at about half continental levels; diminishing markets for uncompetitive UK exports; recurrent balance of payments crises; and poor industrial relations. The UK applied to join the Common Market as early as 1961, once it had been set up, but entry was vetoed twice by French President de Gaulle. UK entry eventually took place in 1973, but coincided with the end of the long post-war boom, as the Bretton Woods system fell apart. UK membership of what became the European Union fell entirely in the post-Bretton Woods era. The early years of UK membership were thus marked not by prosperity and growth, but by monetary turbulence, international instability, and the oil price shock.

Yet, after the crisis decade of the 1970s the UK economy did turn around. As noted by the LSE Growth Commission in 2013, whereas by the late 1970s the UK had been comprehensively overtaken by others, with US GDP per capita 40% higher than the UK's, and that of France and Germany 10–15% higher, the subsequent three decades, from the 1980s right up to 2007 (the eve of the global financial crisis) saw its relative performance improve substantially. By 2007, UK GDP per capita had overtaken both France and Germany, and reduced significantly the gap with the United States.

Membership of the European Union, with its competitive market structures, played its part in this revival. As well as domestic policies to reform labour markets and expand the higher education system, membership of the European Common (later Single) Market brought with it a withdrawal of industrial subsidies in the UK; a movement to effective competition in many privatised sectors with independent regulators; and a strengthening of competition policy. In other words, the supply-side economic benefits which the creation of the Common Market brought to other western European economies in the 1950s and 1960s had a similar, but lagged, effect in the UK. Nor should this really be a surprise: all countries which joined the EU after its launch by the original Six saw economic improvements; from Spain and Portugal in the 1980s to the post-Communist countries joining in the twenty-first century.

Not only did the UK do comparatively well inside the EU, it was able to adapt its internal regulatory, administrative and legal structures relatively smoothly. The writer has advised firms and businesses on competition law issues of all kinds for the best part of two decades, and can recall no case of a serious difference of views between the UK and EU authorities, or between the UK courts and the EU courts. Apart from its political class (on which see more, below) the UK administrative, economic, legal, cultural and educational systems had little difficulty in adjusting to European life.

As the LSE Report also makes clear, however, the fruits of economic recovery in the UK after the 1970s were not shared equally. Alongside improved growth in the three decades up to the global financial crisis came substantial increases in inequality, rising, like in the United States, dramatically from the late 1970s onwards. UK levels of inequality became much higher during this period than in continental Europe or Japan. Behind this lay the UK's "fundamental problem" of investment failure, across the board, from infrastructure to education. As the report lamented, the dynamism that saw the provision of infrastructure behind the growth of the UK as an industrial power had all but evaporated. The UK was home to one of the most dynamic world centres for financial services, but seemed unable to deliver adequate long-term finance for innovation and private investment.

So a two-tier economy developed during the years of UK membership of the EU: parts of it, particularly in London and the south, performing very well, and parts left behind, going backwards, and with no particular strategy or plan to bring the two together. As in the United States, rising inequality was tolerated, and the state saw no role in directing finance towards investment, or countering inequality. It was against this background that the financial crisis of 2008 erupted.

## The Path Not Taken

The retreat from wartime intellectual leadership was perhaps nowhere so evident as in international monetary and financial cooperation. Whereas Keynes, during the war, laid far-reaching plans for a more stable world monetary order—drawing on his own idea of a new "supernational" central bank, at the centre of a network of national central banks (described in *A Treatise on Money*, published as long ago as 1930)—the UK moved in the post-war period from passive onlooker to victim of circumstances, buffeted by the financial turbulence marking the post-Bretton Woods world.

Whereas in 1945, at the end of the war, the pound sterling was worth \$4.03 (the rate fixed at Bretton Woods), it then declined to \$2.80 in 1949 (after devaluation) and to \$2.40 in 1967 (after another devaluation). Following the suspension of Bretton Woods, sterling became a floating currency, and in the 1990s was worth about \$1.50 in the foreign exchange markets. At the time of writing it is worth about \$1.40.

This decline is when measured in relation to the dollar, but within Europe the UK proved equally unable to stick to arrangements for currency stability. After Bretton Woods came to an end, sterling briefly joined a currency grid in 1972 between the six Common Market countries, plus Denmark and Ireland (the "Snake"), but survived no longer than six weeks before being withdrawn, devaluing by 20% against the strongest European economies over the next year.

In the 1980s and 1990s, to combat the growth of domestic inflation, the UK tried, briefly, an informal policy of sterling shadowing the Deutschemark and then a formal policy of joining the Exchange Rate Mechanism of the European Monetary System, in existence since 1979. The UK's forced departure from the ERM, in 1992, after only two years, proved traumatic for the governing Conservative party, and did much to explain its growing hostility thereafter not only to monetary union but to the European Union itself. Yet withdrawing from international monetary cooperation, and focusing on a domestic inflation target, proved again insufficient to avert the global financial crisis, which hit the UK, like other economies, in the twenty-first century.

It is curious to note that the shape of today's European System of Central Banks—with a European Central Bank in Frankfurt and a network of national central banks cooperating with it to run a pan-European monetary policy—bears a striking resemblance to Keynes's "supernational" central bank of the 1930s, designed to work with national central banks to manage gold standard currencies, while avoiding inflation and deflation. And it is equally curious to note that the origins of today's European monetary union can be found in an attempt to create a coherent response to the end of Bretton Woods by a former UK Chancellor of the Exchequer—a certain Roy Jenkins (1920–2003), President of the European Commission from 1976.

In 1977 Jenkins delivered the first Jean Monnet lecture in Florence, and devoted it to the case for monetary union in the European Community. Jenkins proposed monetary union not just for the classical economic reason that it would permit a more efficient and developed rationalisation of industry and commerce, but also to create a better "central economic mechanism" for the Community as a whole. In the wake of the extreme monetary turbulence on the end of Bretton Woods, a stable European monetary system should aim to protect participants from the sword of Damocles of exchange rate and external financial risks, and (as he put it) "penalties inflicted on our people" by a "largely anonymous international monetary system" which could amplify beyond all proportion any ill-fortune of a political or economic nature.

Jenkins saw monetary union taking place alongside measures to combat demand deficiency in Europe (the underlying cause of unemployment), and constraints on policy-makers' ability to cause a "smooth, powerful, sustained ground-swell of demand". To turn the tide, what was needed was confidence in steady and more uniform economic policies favouring investment and expansion; a strengthening of demand with a wide geographic base; lower inflation; and an assurance that spasmodic, local economic difficulties would not be magnified by exchange rate and capital movements into general crises of confidence.

Jenkins advocated active measures to ensure a smooth regional distribution across Europe of the gains from economic integration and monetary union. A system of public finance should provide a convincing insurance for the weak regions against the fear that monetary union would aggravate their economic difficulties; and for the strong regions that they should have more stable, secure and prosperous markets. He cited economic research suggesting that a definitive monetary union might be viable with a rise in the level of public expenditure at a European level from 1% of GDP to 5–7% of GDP. Most public expenditure in Europe would remain with the member states, but the public finance function of the Community would consist of a few "high-powered types of financial transfer", carrying out specific tasks in sectors of particular Community concern, ensuring there would be a flow of the resources necessary to sustain monetary union.

Two years after Jenkins's lecture there came the launch of the European Monetary System in 1979, involving a commitment by participating countries not to let their currencies diverge by a small amount (2.25%) from a central rate. After ten years of relative success in stabilising currencies, and cooling inflation after the inflationary 1970s, the move to monetary union was given further impetus by the 1989 "Report on Economic and Monetary Union in the European Community" (by heads of European central banks, chaired by another President of the European Commission, Jacques Delors). As a result, the Maastricht Treaty of 1992 set up the process leading to the launch of the euro as the single European currency in 1999, and the creation of a European Central Bank at the centre of a European System of Central Banks.

Although monetary union went ahead, it was not quite as envisaged by Jenkins. What resulted was a somewhat thinner arrangement, without the "central economic mechanism" he had in mind. Absent was strategic European public expenditure of the order of 5–7% of the European economy, and the emphasis instead was on member states keeping their own national budgetary deficits within tight limits (no more than 3% of national GDP), and not allowing government debt to exceed a ratio of 60% of GDP. Nor was any attention paid to demand deficiency at a European level, or how to create a "smooth, powerful, sustained groundswell of demand". The economic policies advocated by the Delors Report involved strengthening the supply side of the economy (deepening the single market, and competition policy), with centrally managed Community funds a very small part of total public sector spending. Economic policy coordination mostly revolved around ensuring that member states kept within the rules set for them.

The UK's ejection from the Exchange Rate Mechanism in 1992 meant that it played no serious part in the shaping of monetary union in Europe. Nor did the UK adopt a domestic policy stance remotely resembling that which Jenkins recommended in 1977. Again, it was as if the message of the *General Theory* had been completely forgotten. Privatisation, monetarism and "rolling back the frontiers of the state" became the watchwords, leading in the end to the two-tier, unequal, economy already described.

What if, hypothetically, the Jenkins approach had been followed? As well as benefiting from deepening the single market, an active policy of ensuring sufficient demand would have helped Europe as a whole, and the UK as part of it. "Effective demand", as Keynes put it, consists of both consumption and investment. Jenkins's stress on Europe-wide policies favouring investment and expansion could only have benefited the UK, where investment failure was, by the twenty-first century, its "fundamental problem". Active measures to ensure an even distribution of the fruits of growth across Europe, and insuring against economic downturns, would also have been beneficial. Although parts of the UK prospered very well under membership of the EU, other parts did not, and the weakest regions of the UK took the longest to recover from the global financial crisis of 2008.

It would be pleasant to imagine the UK taking a different path from the late 1970s, and encouraging the global financial system to engage in useful investment, in the UK and across Europe, rather than the speculative activities which led to the crash of 2008. But the path not taken was largely for domestic political reasons. UK politicians recoiled from monetary union in Europe not only because sterling had a track record of instability, but because monetary union appeared to them to involve a complete loss of economic and political independence—the creation of a European Government and the United States of Europe, as a later UK Chancellor of the Exchequer (Nigel Lawson) said in 1989, adding: "That is simply not on the agenda now, nor will it be for the foreseeable future" (*The View From No. 11*). By positing an undesirable end state—not one proposed by Jenkins in 1977, or what actually transpired after the launch of the euro in 1999—UK politicians abdicated any role in shaping events, or creating a better monetary order in the wake of Bretton Woods.

## Back to the Sixteenth Century

We can put the events in this chapter into the context of the rest of this book. As we saw in Chapter 1, Hayek's idea of a decentralised market economy, where prices signal useful and practical knowledge of changing circumstances, came to apply in western Europe once, with Marshall Plan aid, the economies of western Europe revived after the war. By contrast, the economies of central and eastern Europe, under the effective control of the Soviet Union, pursued a centrally planned economic path. In western Europe the economies of the participating countries of, first, the Coal and Steel Community and, then, the Common Market, created a wider decentralised market economy, with strong competition rules encouraging a transmission of accurate price signals.

The UK in the immediate post-war period was certainly not a centrally planned economy like those of the Soviet system, but nor, on the other hand, was it a fully decentralised market economy, allowing price signals to operate clearly. Large parts of the productive economy were owned by the state. Nor was there an active British competition policy, or anything like the rigorous competition rules featuring in the Coal and Steel Community and then the Common Market. British overseas trade remained largely with old imperial preference markets.

After the end of Bretton Woods in the 1970s, coinciding with UK entry into the European Community, two forces were in play. The deepening of the single market in western Europe, and its gradual widening to include not just the UK, but also Ireland and Denmark; then Spain, Portugal and Greece in the 1980s; and then other Scandinavian countries and former-Communist countries from the 1990s, continued the creation of a decentralised European market economy, with an ever greater international division of labour. But at the same time a largely speculative global financial economy developed too, dealing in flows of income from financial and capital assets. This financial economy was not physically located in any one place—although its activities were concentrated in large financial centres, of which London became the largest in Europe. Since it mostly involved trading in rights to *existing* assets, it played little part in creating new capital investment. Pricing in this financial economy was also unstable, and after a series of financial crises elsewhere the global crisis of 2008 hit the entire Atlantic region, afflicting both the United States and Europe.

UK ejection from the Exchange Rate Mechanism of the EMS, in 1992, led UK politicians to query not the "largely anonymous international monetary system" developed since the end of Bretton Woods, but rather the concept of European currency stability and, by extension, European cooperation. In time-honoured fashion, scapegoats needed to be found after the UK's own (relatively minor but traumatic) financial crisis of 1992, and the scapegoat to hand was the European Union. The seeds of potential UK withdrawal from the European enterprise were laid. The long-standing concept of an "ever closer union" in Europe became anathema to a growing section of political opinion (although the European Treaties say only that an "ever closer union among the peoples of Europe" is the objective: hardly objectionable, after two world wars and a cold war). When the global financial crisis of 2008 led to another decade of much more serious economic hardship, and a further widening of divisions in UK society, the scapegoat was exploited again, and leaving the European Union became the solution to the UK's problems—even if on catastrophic terms.

The UK's retreat from Europe was under cover of the doctrine of "sovereignty". This, unfortunately, is an archaic, mystical, doctrine, invented in the sixteenth century by French jurist and political theorist Jean Bodin (1530–1596). It bestows absolute and perpetual power on the sovereign prince, who is separate from the people and shares his absolute power with no-one. It precludes effective international cooperation (because any nation can always invoke its own national sovereignty to renege on any agreement at any time) and so offers no prospect of creating a stable international order. Nor is it of any help when considering how to address today's global financial system, about which Bodin had, of course, absolutely nothing to say.

Jacques Maritain (philosopher, theologian, and contributor to the 1948 Universal Declaration of Human Rights) described in his book *Man and the State* (1954) how the story started by Bodin reached its end once the sovereignty of the abstract entity of the state had been substituted for the sovereignty of the king; and the sovereignty of the state had been confused with the sovereignty of the nation and the sovereignty of the people. It reached its resting point in the absolutist, totalitarian, states of the twentieth century: "That is *just* which serves the interest of the Sovereign, that is, of the People, that is, of the State, that is, of the Party". Maritain's conclusion was that the two concepts of sovereignty and absolutism had been forged together on the same anvil—and should be scrapped together.

So having originally helped write the terms for global economic and monetary cooperation during the Second World War, the UK's answer to the greatest crisis of modern post-war capitalism was to take itself off the stage, withdraw into a pre-capitalist, and indeed pre-democratic, world, and face the challenges of the twenty-first-century armed with an antique doctrine, dating from *circa* 1576. In 2021 the credit rating agency Moody's stated that it expected the UK economy to be "significantly smaller over the longer term" as a result of Brexit.

## References

Gardner A, *Stars with Stripes: The Essential Partnership Between the European Union and the United States*, 2020, Cham, Palgrave Macmillan.

Jenkins R, "Europe's Present Challenge and Future Opportunity", *Jean Monnet Lecture*, 1977, Florence, at Archive of European Integration, University of Pittsburgh, aei.pitt.edu.

Keynes JM, *A Treatise on Money (Vol II, The Applied Theory of Money)*, 1930, 2013, Cambridge University Press.

Lawson N, *The View From No. 11*, 1992, London, Bantam Press.

London School of Economics Growth Commission, *Investing for Prosperity: Skills, Infrastructure and Innovation*, 2013, at www.lse.ac.uk.

Maritain J, *Man and The State*, 1954, London, Hollis and Carter.

UK 2070 Commission, "The First Report of the UK 2070 Commission: Fairer and Stronger—Rebalancing the UK Economy", 2019, at uk2070.org.uk.

CHAPTER 9

# Tomorrow Without Fear

**Abstract** How, in both the United States and Europe, the post-war economic model at first succeeded and then over the decades began to fail. How it might succeed yet again. (The title of this chapter is from a book published in 1946 by Chester Bowles, the administrator of the US wartime Office of Price Administration.)

**Keywords** Arsenal of democracy · Purchasing power · Effective demand · Victory Program · Transatlantic partnership

## The Arsenal of Democracy

The economic fortunes of the UK and the US diverged during the Second World War. The UK emerged greatly weakened: the United States as a superpower, the most important economy in the world. Yet by 2016 the United States, just like the UK, seemed willing to turn its back on the policies of the post-war decades in voting for President Trump. How could a decline in fortunes and confidence reach the point where the election of even a Trump seemed to many Americans a solution worth trying?

As with the UK, the story goes back to the Second World War. It was the wartime transformation of the United States into Roosevelt's "great

© The Author(s), under exclusive license to Springer Nature Switzerland AG 2021

D. Harrison, *Capitalism and the Dark Forces of Time and Ignorance*,
https://doi.org/10.1007/978-3-030-78394-5_9

arsenal of democracy" which finally succeeded in lifting its immense economy out of the Great Depression. It was not so much the impact of the New Deal, or the influence of Keynes, as the launch of a large new defence programme which created a huge industrial demand. Roosevelt in 1940 called for the production of at least 50,000 planes a year, and in the years between 1940 and 1945 United States production of raw steel increased by roughly 20%; rayon and acetate yarn by 55%; fuel oils by 44%; and wheat flour by 27%. Production of locomotives was 560 in 1940; and 3213 in 1945. Production of ships for the US navy exceeded one a day in the latter years of the war.

This vast industrial investment programme not only ended the Depression, and mass unemployment, but created the basis of the post-war US economic boom, and the expansionary policies which ensured no repeat of the global economic slump coming after the end of the First World War. As Porter put it in *The Competitive Advantage of Nations*, the Second World War represented an investment in factor creation of unprecedented scale, driven by the spur of a national emergency. From that moment, decades of research and investment in the United States flowed into technologies like electronics, aerospace, synthetic materials, healthcare and nuclear energy. The expansion included infrastructure, giving the United States the world's premier engineering and construction industry by the end of the war.

The phrase "We must be the great arsenal of democracy", deployed by Roosevelt in a radio broadcast at the end of 1940, was coined by Jean Monnet (1888–1979), working then in Washington as a member of the British Supply Council, coordinating wartime purchases of military supplies (similar to the role he had performed during the First World War), on a letter of appointment signed by Churchill. According to Monnet's own account, he had used the expression at a meeting among friends, including Supreme Court Justice Felix Frankfurter, a few days previously. Frankfurter liked it, asked him not to use it again and went over to the White House to slip it into the speech being drafted for Roosevelt by his adviser Harry Hopkins.

This wartime military investment programme (the "Victory Program" , as it was called) is instructive for the purposes of this book. As Roosevelt put it later in his Message to Congress in 1942: "The superiority of the United Nations in munitions and ships must be overwhelming—so overwhelming that the Axis nations can never hope to catch up with it". Monnet was among those in Washington urging a massive increase in productive capacity, and a memorandum written in 1941 set out the method to be followed. First, decide the scale of armaments needed. Then, second, decide what form they must take. Then, third—and only then—work out how to produce them.

What is instructive about this method? Because a policy of this nature, working backwards from what is necessary, overcomes the uncertainty of an unknown future which hangs over the economic function of investment—the "dark forces of time and ignorance". Once it is established in war that overwhelming superiority is a necessary objective—without which there can be no assurance of victory, or even survival—then investment must be increased to meet that objective. The demand that is set by the scale of armaments needed causes the creation of capacity and—as in the United States—that capacity, once created, can also be turned to peaceful and commercial purposes, as it was after the war.

Does this mean that only wartime conditions provide sufficient certainty for large-scale investment? By no means. But in extreme conditions of war the balance of advantage is obvious: the cost of carrying out a course of action has only to be weighed against the cost of *not* carrying out that course of action. The uncertainty hanging over investment is balanced against the near certainty of disaster if that investment is *not* carried out.

A similar version of the same logic applied to the post-war reconstruction which took place in western Europe. In countries where there was a massive destruction of productive capacity (like Germany), or an obvious need for reconstruction and modernisation after long years of neglect (like France), there was a certainty, or near certainty, that a large-scale investment programme was needed. The advent of Marshall Plan aid ensured it could be financed. In the UK, by contrast, the future was not so clear: indebtedness rather than reconstruction seemed to be the immediate post-war problem, and it was only after the passage of the decades that the inadequacies of the UK capital stock became evident.

Faced with doubts over an uncertain future, the economic risk pinpointed by Keynes is one of ending up with neither one thing nor another: with income which is not consumed, but is saved; and with savings which are not invested, but which accumulate. So the existence of a large-scale and immediate challenge—even an unwelcome one, like war—introduces an element of certainty into the future, around which plans can coalesce.

## A Better Tomorrow, Yesterday

Although in retrospect it is evident that the foundations of US post-war prosperity were laid in the Second World War, this was not obvious at the time. In 1946 the head of the US wartime Office of Price Administration, Chester Bowles (1901–1986), published a short work of popular economics explaining how the policies which had pulled the United States out of the Great Depression must continue if the transition from a wartime to a peacetime economy was to succeed. Its title was *Tomorrow Without Fear*.

The OPA had a relatively good Second World War. Prices were largely kept down during the enormous military-economic expansion, while wages rose and went into savings. Bowles's book—readily available today on the internet, placed there by its fans—takes Roosevelt's dictum "The only thing we have to fear is fear itself" and applies it to the removal of fear possible in a post-war full-employment economy, with active government policy ensuring a wide spread of worker purchasing power through rising wages; and shortfalls in business investment balanced by increasing public investment.

Without mentioning Keynes by name, the book is a highly readable account in plain English of Keynes's theory of effective demand: the need for sufficient consumption and investment in the economy to meet the supply of goods and services. Consumption, said Bowles, would be improved by increasing purchasing power, meaning that the national US income should be distributed as equally as possible, with enough money going to everyone to buy all the goods and services to enable the economy to run smoothly and under full power. This meant getting "a lot more purchasing power" (in other words, "a lot more money") out into the hands of "a lot more people"—in particular those who needed it most and had the most difficulty getting it: "the wage earner, the farmer, the lower-income groups generally".

To ensure sufficient investment, Bowles's idea was similar to that of Keynes, as we saw in Chapter 4: the government should establish a carefully checked file of all necessary public-work projects for which federal funds would be required, to be divided into those urgently needed and those which could be postponed for a year, or for a period of years. Projects would be distributed geographically as widely as possible around the United States. Work on postponable projects would be delayed until such time as an increase in government spending was needed to balance a drop in business investment spending.

Bowles's argument was that only by not repeating the policies of the period after the First World War, and up to the Wall Street crash of 1929, could the US peacetime economy hope to prosper in the decades after the Second World War. He recalled the position in the "tinsel-decorated" 1920s, before the crash: the most business-minded administration in US history, with falling taxes and a government surplus—everything that businessmen thought they needed to ensure prosperity—could still not stop the economy from choking itself to death on too many profits, unless income was distributed around the population to enable it to buy the increasing products of an ever more efficient system.

In the event, there was no second post-war depression. After the Second World War the demobilised US armed forces used their accumulated savings to purchase consumer goods on a vast scale from US industry as it turned to peacetime mass production, and then from the 1950s to buy houses and cars on credit. A steadily expanding market, a steadily improving standard of living for all and only a trifling inflation "seemed to be the new law of nature", as Brogan described it in *The Penguin History of the USA*.

There was, then, a wide spread of purchasing power to buy increased output in post-war America, as Bowles advocated. And although Bowles's mechanism of government investment spending on pre-planned projects to counterbalance fluctuating business investment did not materialise, the advent of the cold war in the late 1940s meant that continuing large US defence expenditure became the norm, and the main element of government intervention in the productive economy. Bowles had advocated distributing government investment expenditure as widely as possible geographically around the United States: the concentration on defence meant a concentration on regions where the defence industry was located. From 1950 onwards national defence expenditure was the single largest component of government purchasing of goods and services, comprising 5% and more of US GDP.

The United States went on to experience robust growth in the post-war decades, and it was not until the first decade of the twenty-first century that a crash like that of 1929 repeated itself, in conditions once more like the "tinsel-decorated" 1920s. In retrospect, several factors stand out. In the first two decades after the Second World War there was a robust and conservative US financial system, still operating under

Roosevelt-era controls. The banking system was dominated by safe government debt—left over from the war—and most US stocks were owned by individuals. From the late 1960s, however, banks became more innovative in creating financial instruments, finance became ever more deregulated and bigger and more unstable, and "money manager capitalism" developed, whereby most company stocks came to be owned by institutional savings funds (like pension and mutual funds, and insurance companies), demanding ever higher share prices, to the detriment of long-term company objectives, including improving productivity through investment.

A watershed was the ending of the Bretton Woods system in the early 1970s, in the wake of which an unstable speculative financial system came to dominate the global economy, and with it the United States, culminating in the global financial crisis of 2008. Inequality too re-emerged in the United States; in Piketty's *Capital in the Twenty-First Century* the striking trend is of a marked drop in income inequality in the United States from 1940 (the onset of the war, and Roosevelt's military investment programme); reduced inequality in the post-war years up to the 1970s; and then from the 1980s a sharp rise once again, so that by the twenty-first-century income inequality came to look like that of the 1920s once more.

These factors reinforced one other. Without broad and rising mass purchasing power, consumption could not provide sufficient demand, and there was insufficient compensating new investment to make up the shortfall, as large-scale collective savings shifted into more speculative activities. This speculation succeeded in pushing up and maintaining high *existing* asset prices, to the detriment of new investment, which in turn reinforced inequality by dividing the economy between those whose income was based on appreciating assets and those whose income was based on production in normal, competitive, markets. "Money manager capitalism" heightened uncertainty to intolerable levels for firms and their workers in the United States: they bore the brunt of a financial system lacking sufficient certainty of the future to invest for the long term in plant, equipment, and the workforce. The crash of 2008 rendered this uncertainty extreme. Tomorrow came no longer without fear for large segments of the population, and with fear of tomorrow came what Minsky had called "potential recruits for an alternative to democracy"—and votes for an exploiter of that fear, in 2016.

## Monnet and Keynes

Jean Monnet said in his *Memoirs* that the day Roosevelt announced the Victory Program, in 1942, was the day, more than at any other time in his life, when he felt the satisfaction of having contributed to a decision that would change the course of events. He quoted a comment by Keynes, as retold by the financial attaché of the French Embassy in London, that when the United States entered the war Roosevelt was presented with an aircraft production programme which the experts in America thought would require "a miracle", but which Monnet was bold enough to find inadequate. Roosevelt came to agree with Monnet's view, and imposed on the nation an effort which at first seemed impossible, but was later completely fulfilled. "This crucial decision may well have shortened the war by a whole year".

Monnet and Keynes knew each other from 1919, when at the end of the First World War each had responsibilities for organising emergency food supplies to the defeated Germany. Their paths crossed again during the second war, when in 1940 Keynes, back working in the Treasury in London, planned ways to coordinate wartime economic and financial resources of the Allies. These included a radical scheme to pool the entire economic resources (gold, securities, raw materials, and current trade balances) of the British, French, Dutch, and Belgian empires, worth some £3000 million, to assure the ability to finance any future expenditure by their war departments. "We could offer the world a staggering exhibition of strength", Keynes wrote to the Chancellor of the Exchequer (*The Collected Writings of John Maynard Keynes, XXII*).

In June 1940, with the German invasion of France under way, Keynes was visited by a French delegation, including Monnet, who enthusiastically greeted a proposal which Keynes drafted on the spot to the effect that, pending the working out of this common pool of Allied resources, Churchill should issue an immediate statement that there should be an association of Great Britain and France which "applies to every sphere, material as well as military… all the resources and all the productive power of each country shall be at the disposal of the other" both during the war and after it, so as to repair wartime damage.

As Keynes wrote in a letter when forwarding his proposal to Churchill's parliamentary private secretary, the French were clear that an initiative like this would be of real help to their soldiers in the "appalling task" facing them in period ahead. If it was felt there was a guarantee of assurance to their surviving widows and houses, they would fight even more desperately. If there was anything whatever in this, surely it was owed them. "It did my heart good yesterday to be in contact with the French", Keynes added, "their extraordinary courage and determination".

A few days later in June 1940, the Churchill government produced—but too late—its extraordinary Monnet-inspired proposal for a complete Franco-British union, with joint organs of defence, foreign, financial and economic policies, and common citizenship. Too late, because the German invaders had reached Paris and the Pétain government taken over before it could be put into effect. Monnet remained in London, and then transferred to Washington as a member of the British Supply Council. Keynes, for his part, focused in London on the financing of the war, and the future global monetary and financial arrangements to follow—which became the Bretton Woods system.

On the ending of the war, Keynes and Monnet had parallel tasks: to obtain emergency financial assistance from the United States for, respectively, the UK and France. In 1945 Keynes led the UK negotiations raising a loan of $4.4 billion from the United States. In 1946 Monnet took part in wartime debt cancellation talks in Washington, and the raising for France of loans and credit for goods amounting to $1.5 billion. But Keynes's early death, in 1946, meant that he played no role in the next great US initiative: the launch of the Marshall Plan in 1947. Monnet, on the other hand, seized on the opportunity to ensure that Marshall Plan aid for France could be used in support of his own investment plan for comprehensive post-war modernisation.

It is impossible to know what might have happened had Keynes lived for another decade after 1946 and, for example, overseen the use of Marshall Plan aid in the UK, as Monnet did in France. It is easy to imagine that his wartime ideas for a common pooling of economic resources and reconstruction would have led the author of the *General Theory* to fertile new thinking about post-war reconstruction on a European scale. This, after all, was the theme of *The Economic Consequences of the Peace*, the polemic Keynes wrote in 1919 on the complete absence of any coherent plan to rebuild a viable European economy after the First World War.

As remarked by Paul Volcker in 2007, in an introduction to an American edition of this work, what strikes the modern reader is the degree to which Keynes's strictures were widely accepted by those in the United States responsible for planning after the Second World War. Policies like the cancellation of Lend-Lease debts, the Anglo-American loan and the Marshall Plan provided sustenance and hope both to the defeated powers and to the psychologically and economically depleted "victors". Within Europe, the establishment of cooperative economic relations, from the Coal and Steel Community on to the euro, contrasted with the fragmentation and antagonism after the First World War.

However, Keynes did not live beyond 1946; the UK failed to use Marshall Plan aid for investment in its own economic modernisation; and the UK failed to interest itself in Monnet's own radical initiative in 1950 to pool vital European coal and steel resources ("the key to economic power and the raw materials for forging weapons of war", as Monnet put it), which turned into the European Coal and Steel Community Treaty of 1951. From the 1950s onwards, boosted by Marshall Plan aid and further cooperative initiatives like the launch of the European Common Market, the western European economies (except that of the UK) grew strongly, with high levels of employment, continuing to do so right until the end of the Bretton Woods system and the first oil price shock in the 1970s. Investment rates, including housing and infrastructure, ran in the 1950s more than one quarter above those of the inter-war years.

As with the United States, the end of the Bretton Woods era was a watershed in Europe. After the inflationary 1970s, economic policy thereafter became focused on disinflation and monetary matters, with the launch of the European Monetary System in 1979 aiming to recreate a Bretton Woods-like region of currency stability. To regain economic growth, the main European initiative from the 1980s onwards was to relaunch, and improve, the common market through developing the European single market programme. This had some, but only limited, success: the growth rates of the post-war period did not return.

And although the European Monetary System led to the creation of European monetary union, and the launch of the euro as the currency for the European Union in 1999, something was still missing from European economic policymaking. As in the United States, policy in Europe concentrated on liberalising and deregulating the supply side of the economy, allowing a better circulation of goods, services, people, and capital (the "four freedoms"), but with less attention paid to ensuring a wide spread of purchasing power by rising wages and maintaining steady levels of investment—or, in other words, the demand side. Forgotten was Jenkins's idea in 1977, when as President of the European Commission he relaunched monetary union after Bretton Woods, that it should be used to create a proper Keynesian "central economic mechanism" for the

Europe as a whole, with 5–7% of GDP being devoted to Europe-wide public expenditure, to counter financial and economic instability.

Like the United States, the European economy was badly hit by the global financial crisis of 2008, with relatively few economic tools to hand to deal with an event both unexpected and scarcely understood. Investment levels dropped sharply, by 17% from 2008 to 2013, accentuating a trend of long-term decline since the 1980s. And inequality, while not yet reaching levels seen in the United States (and the UK) increased too in much of Europe. As the OECD put it in 2017: "High and rising inequality harms our societies in many respects, not least in terms of economic growth. It can hamper social cohesion, results in lost opportunities for many, and can even result in worse health outcomes".

The mixed economy model prevailing in most of Europe attenuated the more extreme effects of modern global capitalism, but Europe alone by no means found the path to prosperity and security.

## Two Unions

From the outset—in a straight line from Roosevelt's "great arsenal of democracy" —the United States supported cooperation and unity between the democracies of Europe. After the Marshall Plan of 1947—otherwise known as the European Recovery Programme—US policy favoured Monnet's European Coal and Steel Community, and then subsequent policies for economic integration in Europe. It was Robert Bowie, a US antitrust expert, who, at the request of Monnet, drafted the first competition law articles in the 1951 Coal and Steel Community Treaty, thus laying the foundation of today's European competition law. And since the 1990s, US and EU competition authorities have worked closely under bilateral agreements and "positive comity" arrangements, with the aim of ensuring that trade and investment flows across the Atlantic, and competition and consumer welfare in the US and European territories, are not impeded by anti-competitive activities.

As long ago as 1962 President Kennedy proposed an equal partnership between "the new union now emerging in Europe and the old American union founded here 175 years ago". This "Declaration of Interdependence" (made in Philadelphia on Independence Day, 4 July 1962) envisaged a united Europe working with the United States to address major world issues like lowering trade barriers, resolving problems of currency and commodities, and developing coordinated policies in all economic, diplomatic and political areas. As Kennedy put it: "We see in such a Europe a partner with whom we can deal on a basis of full equality in all the great and burdensome tasks of building and defending a community of free nations".

Similar views have been held by every president, of both parties, from Kennedy up until Trump. So looking ahead, to the future after Trump, might a revived transatlantic partnership hope to find common solutions to the genuine and serious problems which have troubled both America and Europe in recent decades? Both sides have appeared overwhelmed by events since the global crisis of 2008. And yet, they still represent the most developed democracies on earth, responsible for a large fraction of the world's economic output. The themes of this book might suggest a number of ideas.

The partnership might, for example, aim to repair what already exists, in terms of conditions for transatlantic trade and investment. Both the United States and EU are decentralised market economies, where price signals encourage the efficient production of goods and services. More attention could be paid to removing impediments to trade and investment, and equalising conditions of production, so strengthening their joint economy. This could include updating the competition rules on both sides of the Atlantic, and the rules for subsidising industry ("state aid", as it is known in the EU). The application of the competition rules to the financial and digital sectors, in particular, could be modernised. Recurring asset price bubbles have distorted the transatlantic economy, and represent an inefficient misallocation of resources: joint action to eradicate them could be taken. Currency instability in the shape of the fluctuating euro-dollar exchange rate also distorts price-signalling, and is a further reason for improving exchange rate stability in the Atlantic area, as outlined in Chapter 7.

It is, however, setting the conditions for future investment which is the most important. There is already an enormous stock of mutual US/European investment, with over half of total US global investment outflows going to Europe; and Europe accounting for over half of global investment inflows into the United States. But removing impediments to private flows is not enough to ensure smooth or adequate new investment.

A major item on the partnership agenda, therefore, could be to create the conditions of certainty for the new investment to take place on the scale actually needed to restore the full health of the transatlantic economy. As in the Second World War, productive capacity can always adapt to the new situation, once the requirements are made clear.

The most evident requirement today is to retool the entire American and European economies to meet the demands of climate change. Both are capitalist economies deriving their strength from the industrial revolution, and it is dealing with the build-up of carbon since that same industrial revolution which has now become urgent and essential. Given their large proportion of the whole world economy, joint action by the United States and Europe to remove carbon from their economies may cause the rest of the world to follow suit. The scale of investment required is likely to be very large, and may be of the order needed to reconstruct and modernise European economies after the Second World War—perhaps as much as 5 or 6% of GDP, or even more. But the position is similar to that when faced with uncertainty during and after the Second World War: the cost of *not* pursuing a course of action has become so evident that, once the scale of what is necessary is determined, the enormous transatlantic economy will adjust itself to the new situation.

To do this, the transatlantic partnership could make a public commitment to invest whatever is necessary to re-equip the US and European economies and their peoples for a carbon-free future over a specific timescale, and that the joint resources of both will be mobilised to maximise the effect, and to share the costs, on a basis of full equality.

To assist in the financing of such large-scale investment, there exist large savings funds in the United States, operating under "money manager capitalism", as well as high levels of household savings in Europe. At present most such savings are held in financial instruments, mainly devoted to speculative share price appreciation (as in the United States), or else low-yield government bonds (as in Europe). In Chapter 7, the idea of draining surplus liquid savings, and putting them to productive investment, was raised. For the transatlantic region, a "pool" of savings could be created for decarbonisation investment, subject to joint oversight, aiming to offer stable rates of return to individuals and institutions. Public authorities could help create this "pool", by, for example, issuing special bonds for decarbonisation, and ensuring the physical investment process gets started as soon as possible.

A further joint object could be to reverse the growing inequality of citizens, on both sides of the Atlantic. The means of doing so could be by reinstating full employment policies, and widening purchasing power. This aspect of the post-war economic order has been forgotten, but in

1947 the General Agreement on Tariffs and Trade talked about international relations in the field of trade and economics being conducted "with a view to raising standards of living, ensuring full employment and a large and steadily growing volume of real income and effective demand". A public commitment by the partnership to return to post-war ideals like these would set the frame for reducing inequality.

A practical starting point could be large-scale investment projects to be backed by the transatlantic partnership: income differentials between the highest and lowest paid workers in these new projects could be kept to the minimum justified by the level of responsibility—along government and military service lines.

A major source of inequality is the gap between income linked to the rising prices of existing capital assets, and income linked to production in the economy. Existing capital assets include companies and property (real estate), and if prices rise faster than the real economy a two-tier income system results. Most normal worker income is linked to the output and productivity of a company in competitive markets, but income based on an asset price such as company stocks is set not in competitive markets but in the speculative stock market, which has accelerated far ahead of the real economy. Property and real estate prices, in bubbles and hot spots on both sides of the Atlantic, create new economic barriers and inequalities *within* countries, as property prices diverge between one region and another.

Living off asset prices rising faster than the productive economy is rentier capitalism, and the transatlantic partnership could devote serious thought to its eradication, as harmful to the wider economic wellbeing. Existing capital assets which contribute carbon to the environment are doubly harmful. One answer is to set penal rates of taxation on income from existing assets which contribute to global warming, to encourage their discontinuation, and the shift to investment in new decarbonised assets.

This leads to a further agenda item, which is getting properly to grips with the financial instability which led to the global financial crisis of 2008, and from which the transatlantic phenomena of Trump and Brexit resulted. The immediate response of greater detailed financial regulation addressed the symptoms, but not the cause.

The underlying problem in finance has been too great a shift in the years since Bretton Woods towards "speculation" (attempting to forecast the psychology of the market) and away from "enterprise" (attempting to forecast the actual yields of assets over their whole life). A little speculation is not a difficulty, provided it is a minority activity, and enterprise remains dominant. Savings then are allocated to assets over the long term, encouraging steady investment and companies to grow. But speculation is a short-term activity, and, if it dominates, savings simply switch wholesale in and out of various types of assets, following the shifting moods of the market, rather than being productively used.

The transatlantic partnership could set up a high-level group to recommend practical ways to redress the balance, and encourage a shift back to enterprise, for the greater health of the transatlantic economy. Solutions which work in the United States and Europe—which house the world's main financial and investment markets—are likely to apply in the rest of the world too.

## Stabilising an Unstable World

The theme of reinforcing stability in the transatlantic area runs through such ideas. Unnecessary instability only renders capitalism intolerable for too many. And some of the solutions to the problems faced by the transatlantic area do not exist now—but almost certainly will be found in future. This subtle point emerges from Popper: it is impossible, on purely logical grounds, to predict, by rational or scientific methods, the future growth of scientific knowledge. It is impossible to know now what we might know in future. But there is, on the other hand, every reason to suppose that scientific knowledge will grow. The answers to today's problems of climate change and decarbonisation, even if they do not all exist now, will very likely be found in future—provided there is sufficient time for them to develop, and the conditions exist for them to do so.

So it is keeping conditions stable enough for tomorrow's solutions to arrive for today's problems which is the underlying task of the transatlantic partnership. This requires a certain optimism for the future, and steady nerve, but it is in line with the course of history since the Second World War.

How, if at all, could the UK fit into the picture, if it is no longer in the EU? As a matter of law—currently being reviewed by the EU Court—UK nationals have not necessarily been deprived of their EU citizenship by the withdrawal of the UK state. They may remain, in other words, citizens still of Kennedy's "new union now emerging in Europe". Promoting equality of citizens could therefore be of relevance to them too.

And, despite the formal rupture of Brexit, it seems unlikely that the UK economy will diverge greatly from the wider European market economy, at least in the short term. UK business will continue to be subject to competition laws almost identical in the UK and the EU, themselves based on EU single market rules (and originally drawn up by an American antitrust expert). Mergers affecting UK firms will continue to be subject to the same UK or EU merger control rules, depending on the size of the parties. The UK might attempt to give greater subsidies to industry than permitted by EU state aid rules—but if so will run into EU controls on third-country subsidies affecting UK exports to the EU single market. And if the UK departs from EU standards for goods and services (by lower UK standards), firms will opt to remain with higher EU standards, or else incur the high costs of having *two* sets of standards, for the UK and European markets.

In practice, the UK will remain surrounded by countries abiding by European single market rules, theoretically free to diverge but with limited practical opportunity to do so. It took several decades for its pattern of trade to shift from that of imperial preference, set in the 1930s, towards trade with Europe, from the 1970s. A sudden shift again is unlikely.

A simple aim of the transatlantic partnership might be to minimise disruptions to transatlantic trade and investment flows—including to earnings from existing investments—arising from barriers of a regulatory and non-tariff nature created by the UK which effectively partition the European market. The UK could be treated as a de facto or informal member of the European Economic Area (the wider single market, covering the 27 EU states, plus Iceland, Norway, and Liechtenstein) for the wider purposes of external transatlantic trade and investment. To the extent that the UK continues to comply with the relevant single market rules, so could it benefit from the partnership.

Kennedy's call for an equal partnership in 1962 was made before the UK joined the then European Economic Community, and was intended to encourage it to happen, so that the two sides could go forward faster. A renewed transatlantic partnership might provide the best way of binding the wounds of the departure of the UK from the EU, while also offering new means of improving the economic prospects—and promoting the equality—of citizens in both the American and European unions.

The original point of the "arsenal of democracy" was to defend democracy at the time of the Second World War. In doing so, the basis of the post-war economic revival was created, through a massive investment programme, operating for several decades to the benefit of both the United States and Europe. Capitalism and democracy went hand in hand during this period. But the capitalist system needs constant renewing, as new investment diminishes over time and the growing weight of the past—old capital assets—drags ever more heavily on the future, eventually threatening to undermine democracy itself. That constant renewal—through maintaining sufficient new investment and purchasing power—does not happen of its own accord, as more recent decades have demonstrated. The arts of peace turn out to require no less care and attention than the arts of war.

## References

Bowles C, *Tomorrow Without Fear*, 1946, New York, Simon and Shuster.

Brogan H, *The Penguin History of the USA*, 1990, London, Penguin.

Keynes JM, "Operations on Other Fronts—February to June 1940", *The Collected Writings of John Maynard Keynes, XXII, Activities 1939–1945*, 2013, Cambridge, Cambridge University Press.

Monnet J, *Memoirs*, 1978, New York, Doubleday.

OECD, "Understanding the Socio-Economic Divide in Europe", 2017, Report of the Centre for Opportunity and Equality, at www.oecd.org.

Volcker P, "Introduction", Keynes JM, *The Economic Consequences of the Peace*, 2007, New York, Skyhorse.

CHAPTER 10

# Out of Darkness

**Abstract** Concludes on a more philosophical note, by comparing the growth of unreason in the capitalist era to the problem-solving approach of scientific rationality. It suggests how strengthening competition/antitrust policy might help stabilise finance.

**Keywords** Critical rationalism · Unreason · Booms and busts · Pseudo-science · Competition policy · Antitrust policy

## The Bankruptcy of the Reasonable Man

In his *History of Western Philosophy* (1946) Bertrand Russell (1872–1970) contended that the growth of unreason through the nineteenth century and what had then passed of the twentieth was a natural sequel to David Hume's destruction of empiricism. By this Russell meant that non-rational or irrational philosophies flowered after Hume, in the eighteenth century, demonstrated the bankruptcy of reasonableness.

What did Hume do that was so terrible? He simply demonstrated that no matter how often any event is observed to repeat itself, it does not follow in logic that it will continue to do so in future. That we expect it to do so rests on custom and habit and psychology, but not on logic. This means, as Russell took care to spell out, that every attempt to

© The Author(s), under exclusive license to Springer Nature Switzerland AG 2021

D. Harrison, *Capitalism and the Dark Forces of Time and Ignorance*,
https://doi.org/10.1007/978-3-030-78394-5_10

arrive at general scientific laws from particular observations is fallacious. It amounts to the destruction of empiricism, or the method of proceeding from careful observation and experiment to scientific theory.

It was not until 1972 that Popper published his solution to what became known as "Hume's problem"—the problem of induction, or the formation of belief by repetition. In *Objective Knowledge* Popper turned the question around and put it another way: it is true, as Hume suggested, that it is not possible to arrive at general scientific laws from observation; but it *is* possible to say which of several competing scientific theories is false, by a method of trial and error—by testing theories by experiment and criticism. Scientific "laws" are always hypotheses and therefore provisional: all theories are hypotheses, and all *may* be overthrown—as Newton's theory of gravity was by Einstein, and that was probably the most established theory of all.

So Popper put critical rationalism back on its pedestal—bruised and shaken after a nasty fall. Popper thought Hume was nonetheless right to say we have a psychological need to impose regularities on our environment; to see patterns in the march of events. First in animals and children, and later in adults, Popper observed an immensely powerful need for regularity: a need which makes people seek regularities—which makes them sometimes experience regularities where none exist; or cling to expectations dogmatically; and which can make them unhappy and drive them to despair and the verge of madness if assumed regularities break down.

This led Popper to the fertile idea that expectations arise even *before* any repetition of an observation: they are inborn dispositions to look for similarities, to seek to impose regularities upon nature—even if none exist. Expectations come first: the testing of expectations through experiment, trial and error comes next; and scientific knowledge is created by means of objective theories, communicated to others, and shared widely, which explain the interplay between expectation and experiment.

Capitalism as an economic system depends heavily upon a rational scientific method; but it too is vulnerable to shifting expectations of the future. Economic processes take up a long period of time, and that dimension of time is significant when it comes to additions to capital equipment, through investment. The actual output of capital assets—from Adam Smith's mythical eighteenth-century pin factory to modern airports, power stations and skyscrapers—could not take place without a body of scientific knowledge, accumulated over the centuries since the industrial revolution. But the unique feature of capital assets—that they produce a yield of income in the future, and usually the distant future—makes them prey to fluctuating expectations of that distant future.

The "state of long-term expectation", as Keynes put it, governs whether investment in new capital assets will take place, or finance will be available to pay for it. This is a social convention, arising in investment markets. Within those markets, forecasting the dominant opinion—the dominant expectation of the future—is the key to success. But this self-referential approach creates instabilities and feedback effects, and so capitalism teeters from one crisis to another. Changes in the marginal efficiency of capital—through shifting collective views of prospective yields of capital assets—drag capitalism up hill and down dale. In *Tomorrow Without Fear* Chester Bowles in 1946 looked back over "A Century of Boom and Bust"—the course of American business activity in the years 1845–1945. In *50 Ans de Crises Financières* (2016) former IMF managing director Jacques de Larosière surveyed fifty years of financial crisis since the 1970s. The only material difference is that the first century was national: the second half-century global.

## Crises Without Politics

Societies under capitalism—originating in the developed industrial west, but now fast becoming worldwide—have evolved through a process of gradual, reasoned, economic and political reform, punctuated by crises that appear irrational, test social structures and often open the door to further unreason, if expected regularities completely break down.

Crises of capitalism are indifferent to the political system of the societies they attack. In the UK, the South Sea Company bubble of 1720 predated democracy in anything like its modern form, although it involved speculation and general asset price rises, such as land, in ways that are completely modern. The nineteenth-century banking crises in London, leading to the doctrine that the Bank of England must intervene to calm a panic, were at a time when the state was small: health care for a nervous breakdown of banks came before the state took over caring for the health of humans. The UK was a modern democracy, equipped with a large public sector, by the time of the 2008 global financial crisis: but the effect was to trigger a decade of further economic and political crisis, culminating in a rupture from Europe of incalculable consequences.

Looking further afield, the financial crisis of 1857 which caused Marx to begin the groundwork to what became *Capital* in 1867 involved bank failures across the United States, and spread to the UK, continental Europe, Latin America, South Africa, Australia, and Asia: all different from each other, politically and constitutionally, but united by an international crisis. The crash of 1929 brought forth Roosevelt in the United States, but also Hitler in Germany. The global crisis of 2008 rocked the enormous US and European economies and their political systems. It also devastated the island economy of Iceland; and Communist China was seriously affected too, with recourse to a large-scale domestic stimulus programme in 2009 in response.

## The Shock of the New

As Keynes put it, it is a sudden collapse in the marginal efficiency of capital which is the typical explanation of the crisis which comes at the end of a boom. And within the marginal efficiency of capital, expectations of future yields play the dominant part in determining the scale on which new investment will take place.

Keynes's idea was that expectations of prospective yields are based partly on existing facts which are known more or less for certain; and partly on future events which can only be forecasted with more or less confidence. The state of confidence in the future determines the state of long-term expectation. But because of the extreme precariousness of the basis of knowledge on which estimates of prospective yield have to be made, the state of confidence is never settled: it is perturbed by all manner of external events, and in particular speculation over the valuations of old investments, as they change hands in the stock market. Our ignorance of the future is such that present conditions frame our view of what might transpire several years hence. And decisions affecting the future cannot depend on a strict mathematical expectation, since there is no basis for making such calculations: our rational selves choose between the alternatives as best we can, calculating where we can, but often falling back for our motive on "whim or sentiment or chance".

This is, therefore, Hume's custom, habit, and psychology writ large, providing a view of the future which has come to colonise the world's capital markets. And it is not the custom, habit, and psychology of the individual which matters so much as that of collective opinion, with its own self-reinforcing group tendencies. Confidence becomes overconfidence when speculative stories seize the market about the value of South Sea Company shares; or of land in Tokyo; or of technology stocks: and turns to despair when an entire overbought market collapses, as in 1929 and 2008.

However, as Popper pointed out, while there is no law which allows us to say that future events will always unfold in a particular way, it *is* always possible to say which, among competing hypotheses, is false, by a process of experiment, trial, and error. What remains is the best hypothesis—until some better hypothesis might be discovered, with greater explanatory power.

Suppose we try some competing hypotheses? Would it be correct, for example, to say that yields from capital assets are 100% per annum, and therefore that is what prospective yields should be assumed to be? Obviously not: nothing except a pure monopoly on something unique could possibly achieve such a high rate, and even then probably only for a very short period. Would it be correct to say instead that yields are 0%? Again, obviously not: nothing would ever get built. What about 50%? The evidence is, in fact, as we saw in Chapter 4, that the average pure real return from capital, after deducting operating costs, is over the long term in the 4–6% per annum bracket, and a shade higher for industrial capital assets; somewhere around 7% per annum. This is only an average figure, but it is nonetheless an average in real terms, irrespective of inflation.

Is there a theoretical explanation for this rather surprising constancy? Perhaps there is. The yield of a capital asset is, as Keynes put it, the return to the owner from selling its output, *after deducting the running expenses of obtaining that output*. We could conjecture, therefore, that if markets are indeed competitive the output of a capital asset and the running costs of obtaining it will be subject to constant competitive pressures, and these pressures are likely to keep returns from departing too far from costs. If costs are indexed to output (such as a percentage of rent on properties for management fees) costs will rise as rent goes up. Costs of running industrial capital assets include items like wages, also linked to output. And in competitive markets new and competing capital assets, quite possibly with improved techniques, are likely to come on stream during the lifetime of existing assets, thus eating into their returns.

So as a working hypothesis we might say that prospective yield from capital assets in competitive markets is unlikely to exceed a given annual figure; and experience suggests that that figure is likely to be somewhere around 7%, possibly slightly less or more.

## Why Then Do We Have Booms and Busts?

A plausible explanation is that investors—including banks which provide investment finance in the form of credit—are prone to disregard the near certainty that competition will limit the prospective yields of the assets in which they invest. If the market is a new one, or unfamiliar, the temptation to gain a foothold in it before everyone else, in the hope of higher than normal returns, may be irresistible. Rapidly rising prices of existing assets today disguise the cooler reality that tomorrow's returns are likely to be no more than normal.

Thus, in 1720 what the South Sea Company offered for sale was shares in a prospective lucrative monopoly of UK trade with South America. In the nineteenth century, the worldwide financial crisis of 1857 followed the discovery of new Australian and Californian goldfields—a new source of wealth. Other nineteenth-century banking crises in the UK were linked to the financing of new railways. In the twentieth century, the Wall Street crash was preceded by the Wall Street boom, during which expectations of prospective yields became over-optimistic, propelled by the enormous investments of the preceding five years. As J. K. Galbraith put it in *The Great Crash*: "The 1929 Crash was made inevitable by the insane speculation which preceded it". During the 1920s United States production of capital goods increased at an average rate of 6.4% a year; and the *New York Times* industrial stock price average rose from 106 in 1924 to 415 in 1929. The technology stock boom at the end of the twentieth century was at the prospective dawn of a new information revolution—yet another new frontier, with rosy prospects seemingly untrammelled by competitive constraints.

Since the end of the Bretton Woods system, credit-fuelled property booms and busts have proliferated around the world. This is despite buildings being, as Keynes remarked, a class of very long-term investments where ignorance of the future can be mitigated by long-term contracts and leases between investors and occupiers. Nonetheless, the injection of bank credit into a fixed stock of property (existing assets) has caused spectacular price rises—five to six times in the case of the Japanese bubble of the 1980s. The illusion is that the upward movement in prices—and the high yields (rents) obtainable—will be permanent, stretching off into the indefinite future, and able to survive any cutting-off of credit.

In all these cases, the activity of making reasonable estimates of the long-term yields of capital assets dwindles to that of a tiny minority, or to irrelevancy: what is known, more or less for certain, becomes insignificant compared to the collective sentiment of the market. The growth of unreason in the nineteenth, twentieth, and early twenty-first centuries has not been confined to the abstract world of philosophy.

## Speculation Not so Cheap

Bertrand Russell thought that Hume's demolition of empirical philosophy was devastating. Unless a reasonable answer could be found, he wrote in the *History of Western Philosophy*, there is no intellectual difference between sanity and insanity. The "lunatic who believes that he is a poached egg" is only to be condemned on the ground that he is in a minority, or on the ground that the government does not agree with him (since democracy cannot be taken for granted).

The irrational trends which Russell saw flowing from Hume's sceptical rationalism ran through the centuries and culminated in the clashes of the First and Second World Wars: the second "Thirty Years War", as Churchill called it, when it seemed as if the entire world lost its collective reason. The immediate post-war order attempted to restore rationality and balance to this world system, but not everything could be achieved in a short space of time. Within capitalism since the industrial revolution there has been a germ of the irrational, of the unstable, which if allowed to grow can take the rest of society to ruin.

In resolving Hume's problem, Popper arrived at the idea of "demarcation"—that there is a dividing line between science and non-science. Scientific theories—hypotheses—must be subject to trial and error, or testing by experiment, to see which competing theory, or hypothesis, is the best. A claim to knowledge which is "falsifiable", by experiment, can be considered to be scientific. Theories, hypotheses, and ideas which cannot be so tested fall on the other side of the line, into what he called pseudo-science, or metaphysics. Much everyday human activity does fall into this category: myths, stories, legends, and many systems of belief. Psycho-analytics was Popper's favourite example, since, as he put it, there is no description of any logically possible human behaviour which is incompatible with the psychoanalytic theories of Freud, or of Adler, or of Jung.

Speculation—forecasting the psychology of the market—is such a pseudo-scientific activity, since what matters is current prevailing sentiment in the market, and current prevailing sentiment is constantly changing. If speculation becomes dominant, that means pseudo-science is driving the economy. Almost anything is possible. In the world of metaphysics, almost any credo has been upheld at one time or another by serious thinkers. Examples from the *History of Western Philosophy* are that matter does not exist at all (Berkeley); that the universe is composed of an infinite number of windowless monads, each distinct and reflecting each other (Leibniz); and that all the planets are inhabited, and the most distant have the best inhabitants (Kant).

In the world of finance, beliefs equally fantastical have seized hold of the imagination. In the seventeenth century it was the value of exotic tulip bulbs in Holland. In the twenty-first century it was belief in the occult power of credit default swaps and similar exotic financial instruments to remove the risk of bad mortgages being affected by a drop in United States property prices. At a fatal moment a "falsifiable" approach—that credit, when extended to a group of homeowners, will be reasonably safe provided their creditworthiness is properly calculated—gave way to a speculative, even metaphysical, belief—that, provided the housing market continues to levitate, even those not creditworthy will become worthy of credit. In the end, the banks involved lost their own creditworthiness.

Irrationalism, once unleashed, feeds on itself and is not easy to contain. It has been on the rise again in the wake of the crash of 2008, spectacularly so in the case of the United States and the UK, but also generally, wherever the crash has touched. One of the flaws of modern capitalism is that it is truly democratic: not only speculators in South Sea Company or railway shares, and commercial operators, get their fingers burnt, but everyone, including today the innocent. Political leaders in the United States and the UK responded to the crisis not by attempting to restore rationality, but by trying to throw off the remaining shackles of the post-war international system, to revert to a pre-war state of nature: with trade wars, isolationism and "America First" for the United States; and a return to a mythical past but minus an empire for the UK, in leaving the EU. It is as if the breakdown in the assumed regularities which underlay their economies—the economic certainties on which they were built—have, to paraphrase Popper, made whole segments of society unhappy, driven them to despair and even to the verge of madness.

## The Dimension of Time

However, a rational approach offers grounds for hope, as long as there is the possibility of learning from mistakes. That option remains open to open societies. It should not be forgotten that previously intractable economic problems *have* been solved, and that industrial capitalism has already been reformed to head off the giant concentrations of producer power which Marx in the nineteenth century foresaw leading to world crisis and revolution. Originally in the United States, then in Europe and finally globally, antitrust and competition laws have kept producers from combining, in cartels and other anti-competitive arrangements, and forced them, despite themselves, to compete with one another. This solution was not obvious for much of the twentieth century, when state control of production—or even encouraging international business cartels to fix prices—were serious policy options.

Capitalism consists of production, but it also consists of investment in the capital assets from which production comes. Prices appear to be carrying out similar tasks in both systems, but this is something of an optical illusion. Solutions working for firms active in production do not work when applied directly to firms active in finance and investment.

The element of future time is, moreover, particularly difficult to get a policy grip on, or to legislate for. Production takes place in present time—or over a relatively short-term time horizon. Investment takes place over a time horizon which is long term, and where the distant future is much more important. But how can competing visions of the distant future be made commensurate and brought to book?

Competition policy might provide the beginnings of an answer. Capital assets are used for production, and if producers compete properly with one another it should be hard for long-term yields to be excessive, or to diverge greatly. And if yields are relatively stable that suggests the current prices of capital assets should be reasonably stable too—since, as we saw in Chapter 1, the marginal efficiency of capital is the point where the prospective yield of a capital asset, discounted to the present day, is equal to its current price. But if the prices and implied yields of assets in speculative investment markets become too high then finance will flow to those existing assets, rather than into investment in new capital assets; rent-seeking behaviour will result (living off income from high asset prices); and trouble in the shape of a boom and crash may well be brewing, stopping new investment in its tracks completely if, in a crisis, there is a complete collapse in the marginal efficiency of capital.

In the present state of competition law competing producers are not allowed to exchange information between themselves about their future prices and commercial intentions in the market: it is anti-competitive to do so. This means they are not allowed to coordinate their individual, and differing, short-term expectations. If the price system is to bring Hayek's dispersed useful and practical knowledge together, it can only do so if producers do not agree their prices in advance.

The coordination of long-term expectations—and, in particular, *wrong* long-term expectations—might become a new subject of concern to public policy. Such transactions usually take place within closed financial systems or networks, with feedback effects between intermediaries already interconnected, in various ways. If firms active in finance and investment set prices for capital assets which bear no justifiable relationship to normal long-term yields in competitive markets, what exchange of information—or exchange of beliefs—explains these prices? What custom, habit, and psychology has seized these operators in the market? After all, this is not, in Hayek's terms, useful knowledge. It is, in fact, *useless* knowledge.

What kind of institution might have the standing to look into such matters? Perhaps a public entity empowered to act on behalf of the hundreds of millions of individual savers and bank depositors whose savings and deposits are being handled by firms active in finance and investment. Individual savers and bank depositors are the principals—usually the voiceless principals—for whom financial intermediaries act as agents, and to whom a fiduciary duty is owed.

A competition investigation by such a body might be conducted along the lines of a philosophical inquiry into metaphysical speculation. What reasonable theory could possibly explain a particularly elevated asset price, and how does it relate to the use of that asset for production in competitive markets? If there is no such theory, what exchange of beliefs explains it? Which firms have been involved in promoting it, and sharing it, and why? Who stands to benefit?

If the extension of credit is involved—such as to property—which banks are coordinating their expectations, and is the amount of credit justified by the rents (yields) normally obtained from such capital assets?

An investigation into the relevant financial system or network could be open and public—or closed and discreet—and seek to identify and remove the source of error, as precisely and clinically as possible. The Chairman of the Federal Reserve, William McChesney Martin, once likened the central banker's job of raising interest rates to stop inflation to ordering the punch bowl to be taken away just when the party is warming up. But interest rates affect the entire economy, whereas changes in the marginal efficiency of capital are a narrower matter. Rather than taking away the punch bowl, action quietly to remove a few over-excited visionaries and soothsayers might be better for the health of the party, and the economy in general.

With experience, self-assessment by firms of their own behaviour might even take place, as happens in the productive economy. The results of yields obtained so far from capital assets in competitive markets could be fed back into financial systems and networks, anchoring expectations by basing them on reality.

Extending the reach of competition policy in this way may perhaps lead whole rafts of speculative financial activity to vanish, like metaphysical speculation in the cold light of scientific theory. But if the remaining activity focuses on likely yields in competitive markets an injection of rationality would be brought to matters hitherto prey to custom, habit, and mass psychology.

## The Dark Forces of Time and Ignorance

The future is always uncertain, and there can be no guarantee that there will be continuity of anything. To that extent it is true that, in Keynes's words, the dark forces of time and ignorance envelop investment—and with it every long-term human endeavour. On the other hand, there are degrees of ignorance: some events are more likely to happen than others, and it is possible to construct theories which shine a light in the darkness, and penetrate the future a little way, by explaining why this should be so. Any theory can be overthrown by a new theory, but the new theory has to explain the same facts as before and provide an even better explanation—so the light shines a little brighter, and sees a little further into the future.

Keynes's view of economics stresses the weight of radical uncertainty hanging over crucial matters like the hoarding of money, and the use of unspent and accumulated wealth and savings for new investment. Some of this uncertainty is inherent—it really cannot be removed—and some of it is compounded by social institutions where group psychology and the need for instant action dominate behaviour. Reducing uncertainty to the minimum, by the use of countervailing public measures, whether national or international, to provide sufficient stability—without rigidity—appears to be the key.

But stability for *what*? Perhaps, to go back to Popper, we might say sufficient stability to allow as many possibilities as exist in the present to realise themselves in future. The future exists partly already in the present, and if conditions are right what are mere possibilities now will become tomorrow's reality. As Popper put it in *A World of Propensities*, quite apart from the fact that we do not know the future, the future is objectively not fixed. It is open: objectively open. The world is not a causal machine. It is a world of propensities: an "unfolding process of realizing possibilities and of unfolding new possibilities".

So sufficient stability to allow this creative, unfolding process to take place in its own good and proper time, and without the traumatic crises caused by panics and over-reactions to present-day events, serving only to close open societies down again. Public institutions develop gradually, to solve problems as they arise, and so need constant amending as problems are solved and fresh ones take their place. And since the crises of capitalism are indifferent to political systems, and pay no regard to political or geographical borders, the institutional answers have to be commensurate to the scale of the problem—suggesting an international, even global, approach is necessary.

An international body such as the OECD, or the IMF, might, for example, take responsibility for identifying unstable asset prices around the ever-growing capitalist world, and charge competent public entities with the task of investigating the speculative forces behind them, and the associated systems and networks, on behalf of the end savers and bank depositors located in their jurisdictions.

Is a completely new international settlement needed to banish today's dark forces of time and ignorance? Most of the post-war order, including that agreed at Bretton Woods, still exists. Completely new international agreements are hard to agree, and harder still to ratify. This book suggests that making what exists work better, and filling in gaps in the post-war order through a dose of critical rationalism, would be easier than starting afresh.

What might be helpful to clear the air might, however, be something new and different: something like a truth and reconciliation commission, or a citizens' forum, open to anyone in today's world. In other words, an honest examination of what has gone wrong with the global phenomenon of capitalism, and the practical steps to be taken if there is really to be a better use of knowledge in society.

## References

de Larosière J, *50 Ans de Crises Financières*, 2016, Paris, Odile Jacob.

Galbraith K, *The Great Crash 1929*, 1954, 1980, London, André Deutsch.

Popper K, "Conjectural Knowledge: My Solution of the Problem of Induction", *Objective Knowledge: An Evolutionary Approach*, 1972, 1992, Oxford, Oxford University Press.

Russell B, *History of Western Philosophy*, 1946, 1962, London, George Allen and Unwin.

# Index



© The Editor(s) (if applicable) and The Author(s), under exclusive license to Springer Nature Switzerland AG 2021

D. Harrison, *Capitalism and the Dark Forces of Time and Ignorance*,
https://doi.org/10.1007/978-3-030-78394-5

The manufacturer's authorised representative in the EU is Springer Nature Customer Service Centre GmbH, Europaplatz 3, 69115 Heidelberg, Germany. If you have any concerns regarding our products, please contact ProductSafety@springernature.com

Printed and bound by CPI Group (UK) Ltd, Croydon, CR0 4YY
28/09/2026
02224083-0008